Hidden

Volume IV: Bizarre Homicide

Caroline Bardot

Content Warning: The true crime stories in this book contain graphic descriptions of violent and gruesome crimes. This content may not be suitable for all readers.

Introduction

The realm of murder knows no boundaries, and although it is an unfortunate and dark aspect of human nature, it is important to remember that society rejects violence. We are then faced with the question – if we know that murder is wrong, then why do people kill? Are humans predisposed to become natural born killers because of evolutionary biology? According to science, human's closest relatives, the chimpanzees, kill within their own species to handle competition within their group. Food, territory, and even finding a mate may drive the species to eliminate the source of friction.

John Mitani, an anthropologist at the University of Michigan, stated "Observations that chimpanzees kill members of their own species have influenced efforts to understand the evolution of human violence." (University of Michigan, September 17, 2014). However, if animals kill to eliminate their potential rivals, would that leave the human species predisposed to natural aggression and violence? In short, the answer is no. While animal behavior can provide insight into evolutionary and survival strategies, it is vastly different within human societies.

Throughout the course of our existence, we have developed moral and legal structures that denounce and penalize murder within our own species. We have developed certain social behaviors that emphasize empathy and helpfulness, rejecting violence and creating a peaceful co-existence. If we aren't natural born killers, then why do we kill? Individuals who murder oftentimes have complex motivations. According to the Centre for Crime and Justice Studies, Dr. Peter Morrall, a sociologist and author, suggests that the motivation can be broken down into four 'L's.' Lust, Loot, Loathing, and Love. (Dr. Peter Morrall, *Crime and Justice*, 2023).

Lust murder, also known as a "thrill-kill," is a type of killing in which an individual derives sexual pleasure or gains sexual satisfaction from the act of killing another person. A Loot murder is often driven by financial gain through the act of a robbery, insurance pay-out, or other means to acquire money. Loathing murder is a type of murder that is driven by extreme hatred – an abusive family member, or sometimes a group of people in the form of a "hate crime."

Love murder is committed out of the act of love, sometimes in the form of a "mercy killing" when a person is suffering from an incurable disease or illness. However, sometimes the motive doesn't fall into any of these categories. Sometimes the motive is so bizarre and extraordinary that we are left wondering: why? This book will explore the background and lives of five unique killers.

Armin Meiwes, a German computer repair technician, who murdered and cannibalized a lover he met in an online chatroom named The Cannibal Cafe. Driven by a desire for internet pornography involving torture and pain, Armin's fetish for human flesh led him to post an internet message that said, "I am looking for a young, well-built man aged 18 to 30 to slaughter." Interestingly, the last man to respond to the message would become Armin's first victim, Bernd-Jürgen Brandes. Brandes, a bisexual engineer, under the username "cator99" agreed to be mutilated and eaten. The shocking crime would lead to Armin's comparison as the real-life Hannibal Lecter.

Zackery Bowen, a twenty-eight-year-old former U.S. Army soldier, who strangled his girlfriend, Addie Hall, and then went on to dismember her body in the bathtub. After jumping from the seventh floor of a New Orleans Hotel, police found a note inside his pocket that read, "This is not accidental. I had to take my own life to pay for the one I took." Inside the couple's apartment, investigators found the burned head of Addie in a pot on the stove. Her hands and feet were in another pot, her legs and arms had been seasoned and placed into the oven, and her torso was wrapped inside the refrigerator. The Jeffrey Dahmer style murder would lead to questions involving domestic abuse, mental health issues, and extreme lifestyles in the wake of a natural disaster.

Kevin Ray Underwood, a "single, bored, and lonely" man who murdered his ten-year-old neighbor, Jamie Bolin, after canvassing the internet for death and gore involving cannibalism. Luring the young girl into his apartment to play with his pet rat named Freya and watch cartoons, Kevin smashed Jamie's skull in with a wooden cutting board and strangled her. Once she was dead, he sexually assaulted her corpse and attempted to decapitate her inside the bathtub. Investigators would uncover a twisted sexual fantasy involving torture, rape, and cannibalism through his online blog where he posted under the username "Subspecies23."

Brothers Raymond and Donald Duvall murdered two best friends, David Tyll and Brian Ognjan, on a snowy night in Michigan in 1985. For two decades, there were no answers, and the two men were never seen again. However, in 2003, a witness came forward and recounted a terrifying story that had been overheard in the small town of Mio, Michigan. During a night of drunken rowdiness, Raymond and Donald had beaten the two men with an aluminum bat, pushed their bodies through a tree-chipping machine, and then fed the bloody, chopped up remains to their pigs. The Duvall brothers were known for their brutality and instilled fear around those closest to them using one simple reminder, "Pigs have to eat too."

In all criminal cases investigators strive to find the motive to better under the mind of the criminal. However, not all cases present a clear, defined motive and sometimes investigators are forced to gather evidence, examine the circumstances surrounding the crime, and piece together the psychological profile of the perpetrator. When there is no motive, is the only plausible explanation that some people are just born evil?

Part One : Armin Meiwes – Forbidden Fantasies

"After you're dead, I'll take you out and expertly carve you up. Except for a pair of knees and some fleshy trash (skin, cartilage, tendons), there won't be much of you left."

– Armin Meiwes

Armin Meiwes was born into an affluent family on December 1, 1961, in Essen, Germany. His mother, Waltraud, was nearly forty years old when she gave birth to Armin, and although she was happy to have another child, Amrin would be the third and last child that she brought into the world. From an early age, Armin had an extremely lonely childhood. By the age of eight, his father, Dieter, and two older half-brothers had moved out of the family home. Armin had frequently witnessed the hostile relationship between his parents. They continuously fought and screamed at each other, and Waltraud accused Dieter of being unfaithful. She felt self-conscious about her age and position in life. After all, Dieter was nineteen-years younger than his domineering wife.

When he could no longer take the abuse and slander, Dieter left and maintained a distant relationship with Armin. He continued to send regular child support payments, but he only visited him a few times a year. Lonely and isolated, Armin spent most of his childhood being berated by his mother who had grown extremely cold and callous after both of her husbands had abandoned her. He soon became a mama's boy and rarely played with other children his own age. In school, he got decent grades and appeared to be good at math, but the social aspect never interested him. Like clockwork, after school, he would go home and tend to his mother's needs.

During his adolescence in the early 1970's, Armin's mother forced him to continue to wear outdated clothing including traditional Bavarian-style lederhosen shorts with a white shirt. As blue jeans were becoming the new fashion of the times, Armin always appeared a step behind the rest of the children. If children came over to ask him to play, Waltraud would explain that Armin was grounded because he had been naughty. Instead of being a normal kid, Armin was forced to do housework – wash the dishes, clean the windows, and take the trash out. He became a type of servant in his own home.

Next door to the isolated home where Armin grew up was a family who owned a farm. Here he witnessed their interactions and saw how a normal family co-existed. However, the family slaughtered animals to eat and Armin watched with fascinated eyes as each animal – pigs, deer, ducks, geese were brutally butchered, skinned, and chopped up. He longed for a family, like the one he witnessed next door, and he associated their love for each other intertwined with slaughter.

As the years continued, the longing for love and affection only grew stronger. There was a young boy at school named Frank who all the children idolized and wanted to be friends with. Armin knew that he would never be friends with Frank, so instead, in the darkness of his bedroom, he created an imaginary friend he called Franky. At bedtime, Armin would talk to Franky and tell him all his deep, dark secrets. Secrets that nobody else knew. He confessed that he missed his father and older brothers and that he hated being made fun of at school. Although Franky couldn't talk back to him, Armin felt a sense of peace knowing that he was there to listen.

By the age of twelve, Armin's secrets started to take a dark turn. He told Franky that he had fantasies involving children at school. He wanted to cut them up and eat parts of their body. Franky never judged Armin and he spoke about cannibalism like it was a normal, natural part of his life. In his mind, if he ate someone, they would never be able to leave him like his father and brothers had done years before. The thought of devouring a person's body was peaceful – a way to self-soothe when he felt abandoned or neglected by his own family members.

As the years progressed, Armin satisfied his craving for human flesh by watching gory, horror films. He loved to watch people on film being stabbed, bludgeoned, or ripped apart. He especially loved the movies where the innards were ripped from a person's body. By the time he reached puberty, the thoughts of consuming a person's body, especially boys, started to sexually arouse him. At school, he enjoyed watching the boys play sports with their shirts off and wondered how it would feel to rip their chest open and eat their hearts, keeping a part of them inside forever.

At the age of sixteen, Armin and his mother moved to a spacious manor that had forty-three rooms in Rotenburg. Although money was tight, Waltraud had secured enough money to purchase the spacious farmhouse and she immediately went to work naming each room. Her own bedroom was named "Sunlight," and the room she used to keep her clothing and makeup was named, "Morning Dew." As for Armin's bedroom, she simply named it, "Child's Room."

Even though he was reaching adulthood, Waltraud refused to see Armin as anything but a child and continued to berate and treat him like one. Instead of going out on the weekends to hang out with other teenagers, Armin would stay home and take walks with his mother, make the beds, and tend to do chores around the house. His curfew was strict, and he was in bed every night at 10 PM.

The residents of Rotenburg noticed the odd relationship between Waltraud and Armin. They often wondered why the young man wanted to spend every waking moment with his mother. By the age of eighteen, after high school graduation, Armin wasn't sure what he wanted to do with his life, so he joined the military.

It was obvious from the beginning that Armin would never be a leader, but he presented himself well – he was clean, took orders, and had impeccable manners. Most of his time spent in the military allowed him to stay close to his mother as he was stationed in Rotenburg. On outings with his fellow troop members, his mother accompanied him and even spent nights out with them. The two would share a bedroom on overnights and his military buddies started to make fun of him for being a mama's boy.

Of course, this type of banter never bothered him. He enjoyed his mother's company and didn't want her to be left alone. During this time, Armin struggled with his sexuality and knew that he was different. By the age of eighteen he wondered if he should be interested in women and dating. Although he did go on a few dates, his mother often joined and sat in the backseat of the car. If he brought home a woman or mentioned one inside the house, Waltraud dismissed them and told Armin that the women weren't good enough for him. She wanted all of Armin's attention on her and she wouldn't stand for another woman to be in the way.

By 1991, Armin's military career was over even though he wasn't ready to leave. The higher ups noticed that he would never be a leader and he was dismissed. Armin was forced to find something else, and he took a course from a local college and learned a new trade as a computer technician. He took his first job at a software company called Fiducia and he would travel the region to service equipment, mostly computers and printers, at banks. He continued to live with his mother in Rotenburg and after a hard day's work he would go home and take care of her. He didn't like to socialize with his co-workers but sometimes he joined his male colleagues at a local sauna. Although it was relaxing to enjoy the steam, he mostly went to gaze upon their half-naked bodies.

His new career with computers allowed him to become extremely knowledgeable with programming, surfing the internet, and playing online games. He loved computers so much that he planned to turn the Rotenburg estate into a school for people who were interested in learning about them. With his new lucrative salary, Armin went ahead and started renovating parts of the farmhouse but oftentimes he changed his mind, and he wasn't exactly skilled in the art of renovation. He also enjoyed purchasing old, junk cars and keeping them parked on the front lawn. His intention had been to fix them up and sell them, but he never got around to doing that, so they began to pile up in the yard and rust over.

In 1999, seventy-seven-year-old Waltraud passed away after a battle with cancer and left Armin as the heir to the estate. The enormous house was too big for him to take care of, so he dedicated most of his time to three rooms on the main floor. Soon, the unoccupied rooms were full of cobwebs and dust. The downstairs cellar had flooded and started to attract rats. Due to his loneliness after his mother's death, Armin would dress in her old clothing and wigs and walk around the house to feel close to her. He even dedicated a shrine in her memory.

To help pass the time, he helped his neighbors with chores – mowing their lawn, chopping wood, and helping with any computer problems. Armin, they believed, was odd but harmless. Nearing forty-years-old, alone, and secluded inside the spacious farmhouse, Armin felt something was missing and he went out in search of a woman he could marry and fill the empty rooms with children. However, many of the women he dated weren't interested after only a few weeks due to his behavior and unkempt home. He refused to leave his mother's estate and he eventually accepted that no one could ever replace his mother.

As his loneliness intensified, Armin turned to the internet to research his fetish regarding cannibalism. He learned about serial killers Jeffrey Dahmer and Albert Fish. He was interested in how they had intermingled sexuality with cannibalism. He researched the Uruguayan rugby team that turned to cannibalism after their plane crashed in Argentina in 1972, and the Donner party in the mid-1800s that were forced to eat other American settlers to survive a harsh winter. Hardcore pornography involving slaughter and gore was his preference for masturbation and when the images weren't enough to satisfy him, he created phallic symbols out of food and took pictures of his own penis between two slices of bread.

Armin started to become engrossed in his online research and graphic pornography soon consumed his life. He often stayed up into the early morning hours scouring the internet for more material and when something sparked his interest he would save the file in different folders on his computer. Folders were named, "Meat," and "Terror," where he saved graphic scenes of car accidents and bloodied bodies from being tortured.

In 2000, the internet was still in its infancy and the rise of chatrooms to communicate with strangers was becoming a new way to meet people. When the gory websites weren't enough to satisfy Armin's sexuality, he turned to chatrooms to speak with other people like himself. He was shocked to learn that there were a lot of people like him. People that had a fetish to consume and be consumed.

After coming home from work, Armin would log onto his computer and go into chat rooms. His favorites were Gourmet, Guy Canni-bals, Torture Net, and of course the infamous Cannibal Cafe. Under the fake name of Franky, Armin spoke to other people just like himself. Although, for most of the people he met, their cannibalistic fantasies were only an online game. However, Armin was serious, and he wanted to find the perfect person to sacrifice their body for his consumption and he wouldn't stop until he found them.

Part Two : Armin Meiwes – The Cannibal Cafe

"To bite into your penis will certainly not be easy —
living flesh is somewhat more resistant than fried — but
one thing is certain: our dream will be fulfilled."

– Armin Meiwes

Internet chat rooms proved to be an entertaining way for Armin to explore his darkest desires. He found people from all walks of life – dentists, bankers, doctors, teachers. He was thrilled to find that so many people shared his fetish. Perhaps, he thought, he wasn't so strange after all. However, after spending some time corresponding with these people, he learned that many of them weren't serious, but found it as a healthy outlet to roleplay behind the secrecy of their computer screens. It wasn't long before Armin started his own cannibal Yahoo chat room where he became the master of the content. The online exchanges continued and over time they became more graphic. He admitted that he was looking for the real thing because he was a hungry cannibal.

Armin began promoting himself in the personal columns section of the cannibal forums under the fictitious name of Franky. Here he described exactly what he was looking for, "Seeking well-built man, 18-30 years old for slaughter," and "Gay male seeks hunks 18-30 for slaughter." (Lois Jones, *Berkeley Books*, p. 42). Multiple people answered his ads, over two hundred to be exact, and Armin was forced to spend his evenings scouring through the responses and picking out which ones were serious enough to follow through. In the end, he chose thirty people to respond to and even set up an in-person meeting. Armin traveled throughout Germany to meet his potential victims; however, many of the meetings fell through and he soon learned that not everyone was as serious about it as he was.

In July 2000, Armin began corresponding with a thirty-one-year-old hotel cook named Joerg. In the beginning, the two men exchanged disturbing fantasies about kidnapping one of Joerg's co-workers and slaughtering their bodies. Behind the illuminated light of his computer screen, Armin was aroused thinking about using a stun gun on the potential male victims, butchering their bodies, and filling their open stomachs with mincemeat.

After weeks of correspondence over the world wide web, Armin finally convinced Joerg to come visit him at his decaying mansion. Armin was excited to find a victim to slaughter; however, when he strung Joerg's body into the air using a pulley system, the hotel cook started to feel sick. Armin used a marker to circle pieces of meat on Joerg's naked body – pieces he wanted to remove, cook, and eat. However, Joerg didn't want to follow through, and Armin untied him and let him go.

The entire session was captured on video tape, and although Armin tried to persuade Joerg to be slaughtered, the young man suddenly had cold feet. After the failed attempt, Armin went back online and searched again. He wanted a real victim. In February 2001, Armin received a message from a man using the name "CATOR99." The message read, "I offer myself up and will let you dine from my live body. Not butchery, dining!" (Lois Jones, *Berkeley Books*, p. 44). Armin feared that it was another fantasy, a person wanting to roleplay the fetish instead of following through. He cautiously responded and asked CATORR99 if he was serious because it was something he had wanted for a long time. The mysterious man didn't hesitate – he admitted that he was the real thing and he wanted someone to consume his body.

For the next few weeks, the two men exchanged photographs and graphically explained their tortuous desires. Armin sent a picture of his teeth, teasing him and saying he was going to use them to bite the man's tongue off. CATOR99 replied, "That won't be Hell but Heaven on earth." (Lois Jones, *Berkeley Books*, p. 424). If this was the real thing, Armin needed to be ready, and he immediately set out to turn one of the many rooms inside his mansion into a slaughter room.

He eventually settled on a dark, damp room on the second floor. Years of neglect had left the room dusty, cold, and smelling of decay. It was originally intended to be the smokehouse and Armin believed it was the perfect location for his new room. He set up meat hooks hanging from the ceiling, a wooden cage was placed into the corner, and a long trough was made to help with the flow of blood from his victim. In the middle of the room, he placed an old, rusty metal bed frame with a blue floral mattress and thin quilt. Attached to the frame were ropes to keep his victim restrained. Inside a cabinet next to the bed, he placed a lemon-scented air freshener and a children's comic book about two mice, something he loved to read as a child.

Armin used an old piano bench to construct a butcher's bench. He drilled holes into the wood to allow his victim's blood to drain to the trough below. He grabbed utensils from the kitchen – knives, meat cleavers, and tenderizers to arrange in a neat order inside the room. He also placed his grandmother's ax next to the other instruments just in case he needed it. He proceeded to go through the house and grab as many unused mattresses as he could to help soundproof the room. Of course, he didn't want the neighbors to hear the screams from the torture room.

He used the internet to purchase mannequins to test out the meat hooks hanging from the ceiling and took pictures to display his room proudly on cannibal forums. When his room was ready, Armin sent CATOR99 a message and the two arranged a formal time to meet. However, Armin had strict rules and wanted him to fast for forty-eight hours and only consume water. He believed it would be best to clear out toxins and bodily waste before being eaten.

CATORR99 was the online name for a man named Bernd Juergen Brandes. Forty-three-year-old Bernd had grown up in an upper-middle-class home in Berlin. Both of his parents were respected members of the medical field – his father was a general practitioner, and his mother was an anesthetist.

However, in 1963, when Bernd was only five years old his mother made a tragic mistake at work and due to her error, a patient died. She was overcome with guilt and her husband decided a vacation to the North Sea would lift her spirits. Unfortunately, it didn't work, and by the end of the vacation she had driven her car into a tree and was killed. For years Bernd grieved his mother's death but buried his feelings deep within himself.

Bernd went on to succeed in his studies and graduated from a technical university in Berlin in 1986. After college, he landed a job as an electrical engineer at Siemens AG where he tested software for telecommunications. He was well-organized, respected, and sociable, and soon, after only four years in his new career, he was promoted as the head of his department. All his co-workers adored him and believed he was one of the best managers they had ever worked for. He was responsible, reliable, and extremely knowledgeable in his field, and although he rarely spoke about his personal life, his co-workers did know about his long-time girlfriend, Ariane.

The attraction between Bernd and Ariane was not love at first sight but the two got along well enough. Ariane was three years younger than Bernd and she told her friends that he was easy going, intelligent, and a good listener. In her mind, Bernd's qualities were good enough for a potential husband.

After only one year of dating, Bernd invited Ariane to move in with him and things were going well. Their sex life was normal and the two shared household responsibilities. The only odd thing Ariane noticed was Bernd's relationship with his father. Bernd tended to hide things from him, including his habit of smoking cigarettes. She also noticed that the relationship between the two was cold and distant. Nonetheless, she didn't let it affect their relationship and things continued to move along for the couple. However, after seven years of dating, Bernd and Ariane drifted apart. They would find themselves alone in their apartment with nothing to talk about. Ariane suggested couple's therapy and they went for a few sessions, but it soon became obvious that Bernd was unwilling to open up and be vulnerable.

The couple eventually split up, but Bernd found that being alone was something he didn't want. He immediately went in search of a new girlfriend and scoured the lonely-hearts ads for someone to share his time with. He eventually found what he was looking for in a woman twelve years his junior named Petra. Petra was fun and outgoing and the two got along well. However, things suddenly shifted in 1988 when Bernd confided in her that he was also sexually attracted to men.

The relationship deteriorated and Bernd was right back to where he was before. He decided to search once again on the internet, and he started chatting with multiple women. He bragged to his co-workers about his healthy sex life, but he never mentioned that he was still struggling with his own sexuality. When his relationships failed with women, he finally decided to go in search of a man to see if this would solve his problems. Bernd found what he was looking for at a party one night when he met twenty-seven-year-old Rene Jasnik. The two men shared mutual interests including their shared love for surfing the internet. Rene would become Bernd's longtime partner, but he continued to keep his sexuality a secret at the office. He continued to tell his co-workers about his sexual escapades with women, and although he and Rene moved in together, Bernd admitted that the two were only roommates.

Throughout the years, their sex life was normal – once-or-twice a week and never anything involving physical torture. However, Bernd felt he was missing something, and while Rene sat at home, he drove to the local train station and started picking up male prostitutes to act out his secret desires.

One of his favorite prostitutes was a young Puerto Rican man named Immanuel. Overtime, Bernd's requests became increasingly bizarre, and he wanted Immanuel to whip him until the pain became unbearable and instructed his lover to bite off his penis. Immanuel indulged Bernd's fantasies and incorporated them into a type of roleplay, but after a while it was obvious that Bernd was serious, especially after he brought a butcher knife to one of their sessions and wanted Rene to chop it off. Eventually Immanuel decided that Bernd was unstable and refused to see him any longer. He then moved onto other male prostitutes and asked for the same thing, even offering more money if they did the deed. However, no one was willing to follow through and the prostitutes started to distance themselves from Bernd.

With no other options, Bernd decided to take his fantasies to the world wide web. When Rene left for his shift as a baker in the early morning hours, Bernd would log on to his computer and browse the internet for torture websites. Under the username "CATOR99," Bernd ended up in the chatroom The Cannibal Cafe where he spoke to men who shared the same sadistic fantasies of wanting to be tortured and eaten. He also posted his own online ad seeking men who would consume his body and help him "leave this world." (Lois Jones, *Berkeley Books*, p. 59). Armin spotted Bernd's ad and the two exchanged messages in February 2001. It appeared to be a match made in heaven — Armin wanted someone to consume, and Bernd was willing to offer his body for consumption.

The two continued to correspond throughout February, sharing their mutual fantasies that had started during both of their childhoods. By early March, it had already been decided that the two men were going to arrange a meeting. On March 6, 2001, an online exchange between the two was documented and published in a book titled, "Interview with a Cannibal:

The Secret Life of the Cannibal from Rotenburg," by Günter Stampf.

"Cator99: Hallllooooo????

Antrophagus: Hi, Cator, what do you do professionally, that you are up so late at night?

Cator99: I can't sleep well anymore because of our meeting

Antrophagus: That's a sensible reason. Yesterday I was incredibly tired, it was a stressful day

Cator99: I'm in telecommunications

Antrophagus: Oh, that sounds interesting

Cator99: I believe you

Antrophagus: I'm looking forward to our meeting, it will definitely be really cool

Cator99: I want it to be! I hope it'll be really cool. Are you setting an alarm clock?????

Antrophagus: It's only a few days until March 9

Cator99: Still, I would have rather met you yesterday and felt your teeth

Antrophagus: One can't have everything. There's still some time before you really feel my teeth

Cator99: I hardly know what to expect. Have you slaughtered a man before?

Antrophagus: Unfortunately, only in my dreams, but in my thoughts I do it every night

Cator99: So I'm the first? You have eaten human flesh before, or you haven't?

Antrophagus: No, you don't exactly find it in the supermarket, unfortunately

Cator99: How do you know if it will taste good to you, or that the blood won't make you sick?

Antrophagus: I'm readying myself with my dreams. Once I was so excited I grabbed a needle and drew my own blood so I could drink it

Cator99: And your blood, it tasted good to you?

Antrophagus: It was quite tasty. Once I was drilling some holes and the drill slipped right into my hand, that was a real treat. Blood is the juice of life. It contains everything a person needs for nutrition

Cator99: Then I hope you won't wilt, that you can really see it through without a problem

Antrophagus: To bite into your penis will certainly not be easy — living flesh is somewhat more resistant than fried — but one thing is certain: our dream will be fulfilled

Cator99: But there's not so much in it as there is in muscle

Antrophagus: Yeah, but the penis is principally a spongy material filled with blood

Cator99: For both our sakes, I hope that's true. I hope you have also already thought about what's to be done with the rest. Fulfilling the dream shouldn't become a nightmare for you. No one will know where I've disappeared to

Antrophagus: After you're dead, I'll take you out and expertly carve you up. Except for a pair of knees and some fleshy trash (skin, cartilage, tendons), there won't be much of you left

Cator99: There will be a good bit, like the knees, I hope you have a good hiding place for them

Antrophagus: I'll dry out the knees and grind them up soon after

Cator99: Okay, they're good as fertilizer, I heard that once. I see you've thought about it. Good! Sounds like I'm the first

Antrophagus: And you won't be the last, hopefully. I've already considered catching a young person from the street, but I would rather kill only those who want to be killed

Cator99: That also doesn't sound bad. But yeah, seeing as it's not so totally legal, this is in my eyes better than yanking somebody directly off the street

Antrophagus: Exactly, I'd do it, if it were legal." (*Harper's Magazine*, January 2008).

Armin had been specific in his online ad stating that he wanted a victim under the age of thirty. However, Bernd had lied and told him that he was thirty-six when he was forty-three. Over the past few years, Bernd had become obsessed with his physical appearance after he noticed a bald spot on his head. He had joined a gym and shaved his head bald. He didn't want to lose his sexual appeal as he got older. Now, at forty-two, his once mediocre physique had turned into a well-defined muscular body and Armin was intrigued. The two decided to meet on Friday, March 9th and Bernd awoke that morning with hopeful anticipation.

To cover his tracks, he had wiped his entire hard drive clean and erased any evidence of his website browsing history. He wanted no trace of his frequent chats with Armin and his online ads on The Cannibal Cafe. In the months leading up to the meeting, he had sold his fancy sports car and kept the cash to make sure he couldn't be traced, and also in case he needed to bribe Armin to eat his penis.

As his lover, Rene, slept peacefully in their shared bed he took one more glance around their luxurious apartment but didn't kiss his partner goodbye. Rene was under the impression that Bernd was going to work but Bernd had covered his tracks there as well. A few days earlier he had taken the day off and told his co-workers that he was taking a trip to London to speak to a doctor who could help with his hair loss. However, Bernd had purchased a one-way train ticket to Kassel and made sure to pay with cash.

Armin awoke that morning and started preparing as well. He also took the day off from work and set about his vacant mansion making sure everything looked nice, especially his torture chamber where the two would be most active. He swept his fingers across various torture devices to make sure they were sharp. He also went to the local store and purchased items including red wine, brussels sprouts, potatoes, and coffee. As he cleaned and tidied the rooms, Armin hoped this was the real thing, the thing he had been dreaming of since he was a young boy.

Part Three : Armin Meiwes – The Torture Chamber

"The first bite was, of course, very strange."

– Armin Meiwes

The train ride to Kassel took Bernd just under three hours and Armin was already on the platform waiting for him when he arrived. Although the two had never met, they recognized each other instantly. As they got into Armin's car, Bernd suggested that they stop at a local pharmacy to purchase pain medication to help ease the pain during his slaughter.

Armin had cold medicine with alcohol that could help knock him out, but Bernd wanted to make sure he was unconscious so the two bought sleeping pills and a large bottle of Schnapps. Bernd re-entered Armin's car with a new feeling of dread – not because he was about to be devoured but because he hadn't eaten in two days. He tried to focus on the activity outside the car window and he watched local shoppers go in-and-out of stores and took a note of how beautiful the town looked as they continued to drive through the countryside to Armin's secluded estate.

The drive back to Armin's house took over an hour and while the two had the chance to chat, Armin knew this was the real deal. Bernd was ready to become his victim. As Armin's wheels hit the gravel driveway, Bernd was in awe at the size of the house. He couldn't believe that Armin lived alone on such a massive estate. The two quickly went inside and Armin showed Bernd around the out-of-date house. Armin reminded Bernd that he wanted to keep the house as it was after his mother died. Bernd, used to living in the luxury of a modern apartment complex, couldn't believe how old fashioned, dusty, and enormous it felt inside. For a moment he let it all sink in that this would be home where he would be eaten alive.

Armin excused himself and went to make the two a cup of coffee. When he returned, he found Bernd inside the living room sitting on a chair completely naked. Bernd wanted Armin to see him in his entirety, allowing his eyes to gaze upon his next meal. Of course, Armin wasn't appalled by Bernd's naked body. It was fit and toned for a man of forty-three and he was immediately aroused thinking about sinking his teeth into Bernd's muscular shoulders and thighs. Bernd wanted Armin to "admire his dinner." (*Evidence Locker,* 2023). Bernd suggested Armin strip down so he could look at his body, which he did, and the two sat together in the living room casually sipping their coffee and exchanging stories about cannibalism. After some time, Armin wanted to show Bernd his slaughter room and the two went upstairs where they engaged in sexual intercourse for the first time.

When it was over, Bernd told Armin that he didn't enjoy it because Armin had been too gentle. As a masochist, Bernd wanted to be man-handled, he reveled in the pain and torture of sexual ecstasy. He wanted more, and this time, as he once again became aroused thinking about Armin biting into his flesh, he instructed his new lover to take a bite out of his penis. He had waited long enough and wanted to fulfill his ultimate fantasy.

Armin had fantasized about this exact moment for years but when it was time to do it, he froze. He couldn't bring himself to bite down hard enough to satisfy his partner. Armin attempted to chomp down as Bernd screamed for him to make the blood gush from his member, but he still wasn't ready. Instead, he ran downstairs to the bathroom and grabbed a bottle of Wicks MediNait to make Bernd drowsy. Perhaps if Bernd was sedated it would be easier to inflict the amount of pain he so desperately craved.

Back upstairs, Armin handed the bottle to Bernd and he chugged it quickly hoping it would take effect fast. Unfortunately, after thirty minutes, Bernd wasn't feeling a thing, and he began to think that Armin wasn't the man for the job after all. Disappointed, Bernd told Armin that he wanted to go back to the train station so he could go home to Berlin. Although he wasn't happy to allow his victim to leave, Armin turned off the video camera that recorded them and the two got dressed and went back into Armin's car headed for Kassel station. During the drive, Armin continued to try to seduce Bernd saying that if the two went back he would be aggressive in his approach, but Bernd didn't believe him. He was beginning to believe that no one would ever be able to fulfill his darkest fantasies.

At the train station, Bernd purchased another one-way ticket back to Berlin while Armin continued to persuade him to return to the slaughterhouse. He promised that if he returned, he would devour every inch of his body as he had become aroused just thinking about it. Bernd excused himself and went into the bathroom. He was dizzy from the forty-eight-hour fast combined with an entire bottle of cold medicine. He went to the sink and splashed cold water over his face to wake himself up. Inside his mind, he debated what he should do – he thought that this might be his only chance to have his desires fulfilled. After returning from the bathroom, he sat back down next to Armin and said he wanted to try again.

On the way back to Armin's estate, the two men stopped again and bought another bottle of cold medicine and a box of sleeping pills. Back in the car, Bernd chugged the bottle and popped ten sleeping tablets hoping that by the time they returned he would be subdued enough for Armin to feel comfortable with his castration. As the two drove back, Bernd stared out the window waiting for the sedation to hit, and his thoughts went back to his partner in Berlin. He wondered if he was worried that he didn't return home from work and when he would start reaching out to their mutual friends asking if they had seen him. For a moment he felt sad about leaving his partner, but quickly returned to the present and looked forward to being completely devoured by the man sitting next to him. He hoped this time Armin would follow through on his promise.

When the two returned to Armin's house, they both went immediately into the slaughter room where Bernd lay on the bed. He was now feeling a bit dizzy and drunk from the cold medication and in a stupor, he told Armin, "Castrate me. Then kill me. Now." (Lois Jones, *Berkeley Books*, p. 97). Armin, now fully aroused, turned the camera back on so the two could watch the castration later and grabbed one of the kitchen knives that was arranged in the room and walked back towards his victim. Bernd was excited as he watched Armin come closer with the knife.

Although he wanted Armin to bite it off, a kitchen knife would ensure a clean cut. Placing Bernd's penis on a bread box, Armin lifted the knife and struck down as hard as he could; however, nothing happened. Bernd's penis was still attached. He tried again but nothing. Bernd suggested Armin go downstairs to the kitchen for a sharper knife. Used to taking orders from his mother, Armin left immediately and went in search of a sharper tool.

He returned a few moments later with a chopping knife and this time he had checked to make sure it was sharp enough to finish the job. Once again, he placed Bernd's penis in position and struck down as hard as he could. Bernd immediately screamed in pain as the blade cut through his body. He twisted and rolled on the bed as blood gushed from the wound.

Armin struck him again and again until the entire penis was severed, feeling a warm rush throughout his body as he watched Bernd's agonized look of pain in combination with the blood and gore in front of his eyes. Bernd was surprised that it didn't hurt as badly as he thought but as the blood gushed on the mattress and down his thighs, he knew that it would need to be bandaged so he could enjoy the feast with Armin.

Armin bandaged the stump as best he could and took the penis downstairs to cook. He licked the blood from the member and cut it down the middle and sauteed it for a few minutes over high heat. He returned upstairs with two pieces for each of them arranged on his mother's best China. Unfortunately, the meat was too tough to eat, and Armin returned downstairs where he added salt, pepper, and garlic powder to the member and threw it back on the frying pan. As he cooked the two pieces of meat it began to shrivel and turn black making it inedible for either man to consume. Instead, he cut the rest of the penis up into smaller pieces and fed it to his dog. He returned to his victim and told him the bad news but assured him that they could eat his testicles in the morning for breakfast.

By this time, Bernd was beginning to feel lightheaded and weak from the blood loss and asked Armin to run him a warm bath so he could relax and soak. Being the proper host he was, Armin obliged and helped Bernd step into the dirty tub. After his mother's death, Armin never bothered to clean the bathroom and now a dark gray ring of filth surrounded the white tile; however, Bernd didn't mind and allowed his body to sink deep into the water.

Bernd continued to slip in-and-out of consciousness as the gray bath water turned bright red. By this time, Bernd had lost a significant amount of blood, and he could feel his body become weightless within the water. He knew it was only a matter of time before death came for him and he was ready. Armin continued to check on Bernd every fifteen minutes in the bath in-between reading a Star Trek novel in the next room. Every time he came in, a weird smile was on Bernd's face and Armin would later admit it was probably because Bernd was in a pool of his own blood. After three hours in the tub, Bernd called for Armin to help him out. He was now extremely weak and could hardly remember what was going on at all. He scanned the room for any signs of familiarity and when he saw Armin's face he suddenly remembered where he was and what was going on. All he wanted was to go lie down and go to sleep; however, when he tried to stand up, he collapsed on the floor and Armin was forced to drag his body into the next room and place him on the bed.

For the next few hours, Bernd lay helpless on the bed as his pulse slowed, inching every minute near death. For Armin, his death felt like an eternity. Bernd had had his fun and now the butchering of the body was what Armin longed for, but he couldn't do it until Bernd was dead. Before he slipped into a state of unconsciousness, Bernd had given Armin detailed instructions on what to do – once his pulse was weak and he was no longer responsive, Bernd had told him to drive a knife deep into his neck to finish the job.

At 3:30 AM, Armin returned to the bedroom to check on Bernd and found him cold to the touch and not responding. He slowly lifted an eyelid and snapped his fingers loudly in Bernd's ear. No response. Armin grew excited with the anticipation that it was now his turn for sexual satisfaction. He immediately ran to his bedroom to change out of his pajamas and into his slaughter outfit – a pair of loose-fitting blue pants, a pair of Wellington boots, and an old bed sheet that had been ripped to serve as an apron.

He returned to the slaughter room and turned on the video camera to record himself. Of course, the video wasn't meant to be sold, it would just be a way for Armin to remember what he had done so he could go back and watch. With as much strength as he could muster, he lifted Bernd's limp body from the bed and carried it to the slaughter bench, arranging his arms and legs so they were stretched out and his face was turned towards the ceiling.

Bernd's breathing was shallow, and his lips were slightly parted. He then decided to say a silent prayer to God and ask for forgiveness as the killing part was the part that he didn't want to do. If only Bernd had killed himself, it would have made this whole situation easier, but unfortunately, he would have to be the one to do it. He leaned down and kissed Bernd on the mouth and said goodbye before plunging a long kitchen knife into his neck a total of three times. Blood oozed from the wound and began to drip onto the floor. It had taken Bernd nine-hours-and-thirty-minutes to die after his castration. Once Bernd was dead, Armin stared at the body on the table with a newfound feeling of power and accomplishment. His dream had finally come true.

Part Four : Armin Meiwes – Gein Configuration

"The flesh tastes like pork but stronger."

– Armin Meiwes

Bernd was dead and it was now time for him to be hoisted upside down on the meat hook to allow the body to completely drain of its remaining blood. In the fetish world of cannibalism, this is referred to as the Gein configuration. The victim's arms are tied behind their back to allow the butcher easy access to the torso of the body. First, Armin used the knife to cut across Bernd's throat, allowing the deep cut to completely rid any blood left inside the body.

Watching the red stream ooze from the wound excited Armin and he quickly grabbed a bucket to catch as much as he could to avoid a lengthy cleanup. He then sliced through the remaining muscles and ligaments to fully remove the head. He decided he wouldn't eat the brain as he had heard it wasn't good to eat. Instead, he decided to keep it so Bernd could watch the remainder of the butchering and placed it on a nearby table.

Next, Armin began to skin his victim. He had watched multiple videos and knew how to precisely cut through the two layers of skin. He cut long, vertical slices about an inch apart and carefully peeled away the skin, revealing a layer of fat beneath the surface. Once the skinning portion was complete, he disemboweled Bernd, careful not to cut any internal organs in the process. He scooped out the intestines, liver, and stomach and enjoyed how slippery they felt in his hands. The butchering part of the act had made him feel extremely powerful, like he was the most important man in the world. Once all the internal organs were removed, Armin then used a saw to dismember his victim. First, he cut the arms by the shoulder and then cut each piece into sections at the elbow joint and hand. He removed the spinal cord by cutting through the tailbone and finished by removing the legs and cutting those into three pieces as well.

Finally, Armin was ready to remove the cuts of meat he wanted to eat – the calf, thigh, and rump. The entire process was grueling work and took hours to complete. The parts he wanted to eat were divided up and packaged into meal-size portions that would be put into the freezer. As for the rest of the body, he took it out into the neglected garden in the backyard and dug a hole to bury it. Before discarding the contents of Bernd's body into the shallow grave, he made sure to recite a prayer. It was Psalm 23 and it had always been one of his favorites. In a low voice he said aloud, "The Lord is my shepherd; I shall not want. He maketh me lie down in green pastures: he leadeth me beside the still waters." (Lois Jones, *Berkeley Books*, p. 126).

Armin couldn't help but wonder if what he had done would send him to the deepest depths of hell. He hoped he would be forgiven as he slowly placed the leftover parts of Bernd's body into the grave. After one final prayer, he slowly shoveled the soil on top of the grave and said one last farewell to his victim.

Back inside, Armin went to work labeling the contents of the meat he wanted to freeze. There were cuts that read, "steak," "fillet," "bacon," and "ham." (Lois Jones, *Berkeley Books*, p. 126). He was excited to try his first meal and settled on a rump steak that had been butchered from Bernd's back. He paired it with princess potatoes, brussels sprouts, and a glass of South African red wine.

In a later interview he admitted, "I decorated the table with nice candles. I took out my best dinner service and fried a piece of rump steak – a piece from his back – made what I call princess potatoes, and brussels sprouts. After I prepared my meal, I ate it. The first bite was, of course, very strange. It was a feeling I can't really describe. I'd spent over 40 years/30 years longing for it, dreaming about it. And now I was getting the feeling that I was achieving this perfect inner connection through his flesh. The flesh tastes like pork but stronger, more substantial. Although I don't think that other people would have noticed the difference, had they eaten it. It tasted really good." (*Evidence Locker*, 2023).

He also decided to experiment with Bernd's arm and foot. Inside the oven, he baked the arm to dry it out but when it shriveled and didn't appear appetizing, he used his grinder to grind it up and make flour. He stashed it inside of an old bread bin to be used later.

As for the foot, he had no desire to eat it but rather boil it in a pot and cook it over the stove top. Once he was finished, he decorated it with ketchup and surrounded it with herbs in a bizarre ritual to make it appear aesthetically pleasing.

He finished the day by going back and re-watching the four-hour recording of his butchering job. He became sexually aroused once again as he watched himself pull Bernd's innards out of his body and he kept pausing the best parts to masturbate. Over the next two days he ate different parts of Bernd's body, making sure to bring his head downstairs so he could enjoy the moment. For inspiration, he browsed the internet for recipes and even went through his mother's old cookbooks to find tasty meals. Meanwhile, he went back to his computer in search of another victim.

Armin would end up consuming over forty-five pounds of Bernd's flesh over a ten-month timespan. However, back in Berlin, Bernd's lover, Rene, was growing concerned when Bernd didn't arrive home from the office on the evening of March 9th. It was odd for Bernd not to return home at all. He figured that he met up with some friends and would be back when he woke up in the morning. Unfortunately, when he rolled over in bed to hug his partner when he woke up, Bernd still wasn't there.

Now concerned, he phoned friends and co-workers who might know where his lover was but everyone, he called was no help. No one had seen or talked to Bernd at all. By the morning of Monday, March 12th, Rene was in a panic and phoned Bernd's place of employment to see if he had shown up that morning. Of course, they informed Rene that Bernd hadn't shown up and also, he had taken the previous Friday off. Rene was upset that Bernd never mentioned that to him. Now worried, he decided to phone the police, but they did not appear to be overly concerned. They had seen missing lovers before that often involved another person, a relationship squabble, or simply a breakdown in the relationship. Unfortunately, Rene was getting nowhere in his search.

Rene decided to do his own police work and realized that Bernd's bank account had no recent transactions – Bernd had made sure to cover all the tracks that led to Armin and his death. After a few weeks, there was still no sign of Bernd, and the police were also getting nowhere in their search. With no information, Rene was forced to consider the realization that perhaps Bernd had committed suicide.

Meanwhile, Armin was quickly eating the meat he had taken from Bernd's body and needed another victim to supply his stash. He continued to speak with other cannibals inside The Cannibal Cafe chat room using names such as Eaten Up and Gourmet. During one email exchange, Armin had admitted to another user, "I hope to find another victim soon because flesh is everything." (Lois Jones, *Berkeley Books*, p. 146). He also posted advertisements for a new victim saying, "Slaughter boy sought. Are you between 18 and 25 years old, healthy with a normal build? Do you want to end your life, but you want something decent to come out of you, then come to me. I will slaughter you and worship your body, in delicious schnitzel and steaks. Those interested should apply with details of age, height and weight, ideally with a photo. Franky, the master butcher." (Lois Jones, *Berkeley Books*, p. 146).

Armin received a few replies, but nobody was serious enough to meet him in person. Like before, many of the people in the chatroom were only willing to go as far as roleplaying and Armin was frustrated that nobody was willing to offer their real bodies for him to consume. Of course, he wasn't a serial killer and didn't want to go out and find victims against their will. He thoroughly enjoyed the butcher only if he had a willing victim. Someone who had the desire to be eaten just as Bernd had. To attract more attention to himself, Armin grew bolder inside The Cannibal Cafe chatroom and, as his alter-ego Franky, shared with other members that he had in fact killed and eaten a man. Little by little he shared his darkest secrets with other strangers. Once he started to share, he found it difficult to stop. Something about reliving the details aroused him and soon others noticed.

On the evening of July 9, 2001, an Austrian medical student named Reinhold H. came across Franky's advertisement on The Cannibal Cafe. The student was curious about cannibalism, although it wasn't his fetish of choice. He decided to send a message to Armin and the two started up a conversation about cannibalism. Armin was extremely graphic in his chat and Reinhold pushed it further by offering himself as his next potential victim.

Armin was fascinated with the young man and admitted that he would be perfect – he was young which meant his meat would be extremely tender and delicious to eat. Although Reinhold just played along with the fantasy and never had any intention of acting upon it, Armin wanted him to know he was the real deal. During one of their final email exchanges, Armin sent Reinhold graphic photographs and told the young man that he had already killed somebody and wanted to do it again. Disgusted with what he saw, he deleted his email address and account within The Cannibal Cafe. He was frightened and didn't want Franky to come after him.

Although Reinhold was nervous about outing himself on the forums due to the potential of being expelled from medical school for misconduct, he believed that the authorities should be alerted to the potential dangers of what Franky could do. He decided to call the Federal Criminal Police Office in Wiesbaden and tell them what had happened. During the phone call, he stressed that he would help as much as he could in the investigation, but he wasn't willing to speak out during a court case. He was scared and disgusted with himself for even speaking to Franky about cannibalism and now he wanted to help but he also wanted to keep his distance.

The police thanked him for the information and promised they would follow up on his tip. It would be another two months before the police discovered that Franky was a man named Armin Meiwes, and another five months before they obtained a search warrant to search his property.

On December 10, 2001, around 8:45 AM, Armin was awoken to the sound of persistent knocking on his front door. When he answered it, he was shocked to find multiple police officers informing him they were armed with a search warrant regarding a tip he had killed and eaten a man. Armin invited them inside the dilapidated manor and offered them coffee. Police officers noticed he was calm and welcoming. He didn't fit the description of a cannibal killer. The police stated that they had received an anonymous tip regarding his interactions with other people on cannibal fetish websites and one asked him directly, "Have you eaten human flesh, Mr. Mewies?" He responded, "I may have." (Lois Jones, *Berkeley Books*, p. 160). Now suspicious, the police officers went to work and thoroughly searched the house for any evidence. They found multiple documents on his computer that showed his obsession with violent pornography, torture, and cannibalism. Inside the chest freezer they located multiple stacks of meat and located a false bottom inside. They uncovered thirty-five pre-packaged portions of unique-looking meat, something they had never seen before. When they asked Armin what type of meat it was, he told them it was meat from a wild pig.

Of course, the police didn't believe him as the evidence continued to mount up. The only thing they could do was confiscate the meat and test it for DNA. After confiscating the contents of the freezer, they walked upstairs and discovered the slaughter room. The meat hooks, knives, and trough designed for slaughtering a body were disgusting and strange, but it didn't mean that Armin actually killed a person. The only thing they could charge him for now before any DNA evidence was "glorification of violence." (Lois Jones, *Berkeley Books*, p. 162).

When they left, the police had confiscated Armin's computer, an ax, multiple knives, a butcher's apron, and the meat from the freezer. They did not have the video tape of Bernd's slaughter, as Armin had made sure to hide his secret. The police did not have enough evidence to arrest him and had to wait for DNA testing to determine who the meat belonged to.

After the police left his residence, Armin knew that it was only a matter of time before his dark secret would be discovered. He immediately dialed a local attorney named Harald Ermel – the same man he had used for a minor offense years earlier involving drunk driving. This time, however, the crime was more serious and when Harald asked what happened, Armin admitted that he had killed and eaten another man.

Harald was shocked by what he had just heard and told his client that the best course of action would be to turn himself in. Shockingly, Armin agreed and when the two hung up Harald immediately dialed the local police and told them about his confession. Later that day, the police arrived at Armin's estate and arrested him. He was taken into custody around 5 PM and made a full confession to the police.

The next day, he remained cooperative and accompanied the police back to his residence and told them the whole story. He almost seemed proud of his cannibalistic obsessions and even pointed out the bread box where he kept Bernd's ground up bones he intended to use for flour. He admitted that the man he killed was a gay man he met in a chat room named Bernd and willingly gave them the four-hour videotape of Bernd's slaughter. Detective Wilfried Fehl was given the job of watching and evaluating the video. Meanwhile, the police were back at work searching for more evidence on Armin's property. This time, through the help of a cadaver dog, they located a shallow grave that contained human bones. DNA testing would later confirm that the bones and meat belonged to Bernd-Jürgen Brandes.

What remained of Bernd was given back to his loved ones in Berlin and cremated. When Bernd's father learned about his son's death, he refused to attend the funeral that his lover, Rene, had organized. Instead, only a handful of Bernd's closest friends attended the private ceremony to honor and remember him. Meanwhile, Armin was in jail and state psychiatrists were brought in to speak with him. They learned that Armin's cannibalistic fantasies started at a young age as a way to consume a person and have them become a part of him. Armin admitted that after eating Bernd he felt he had filled a void within himself and said, "I got a kick out of the idea of having another person inside of me. I had the fantasy, and, in the end, I fulfilled it." (Lois Jones, *Berkeley Books*, p. 173). However, Armin was adamant that he didn't murder Bernd but rather assisted him in suicide. After reviewing the videotape, German officials believed that Bernd died due to having his throat slit and wanted Armin to be charged with murder.

For one year, Armin sat in a high security prison while he waited for his trial to start. On December 3, 2003, Armin arrived in court for his trial, and he appeared calm and smug. He didn't believe that he would be convicted of murder.

The evidence was all contained on the videotape which showed Bernd as a willing victim. Armin even took the stand in his own defense and spoke about his childhood and how his father neglected and abandoned him, his obsession with horror and gore, and the fantasies involving cannibalism beginning at the young age of eight. He walked the jury through the events that led up to Bernd's death – how the two met on the internet, Bernd's second thoughts about going through with it, and the detailed, graphic testimony of cutting his penis off, putting it in the frying pan, and being unable to eat it. He even admitted, "If I hadn't been so stupid as to keep looking on the Internet... I would have taken my secret to the grave." (*Evidence Locker*, 2023).

Of course, the graphic video tape was not shown in its entirety to the jury. They were allowed to watch nineteen minutes of it, and many became physically ill, and some even needed therapy after watching it. Armin pleaded before the certain contents of the video were shown saying, "It wasn't murder; it was a mercy killing. didn't want to kill anybody or cause pain." (*UPI*, December 9, 2003).

On January 30, 2004, Armin was found guilty of the lesser offense of manslaughter and sentenced to eight-and-a-half-years in prison with the judge saying that although the killing was "viewed with revulsion" the evidence presented, "This is manslaughter, killing a person without being a murderer. The famous lust for murder was not there. There were no base motives." (Lois Jones, *Berkeley Books*, p. 198). Amin was satisfied enough with the ruling. He figured since he had been a model prisoner that he would only serve five years at most and get out without having a murder conviction over his head. However, many people disagreed with the verdict, including Bernd's friends, family, and co-workers, and many people who knew Armin in Rotenburg. They feared that if Armin was released, he would kill again.

In April 2005, the court of appeals reversed Armin's conviction and this time, the Germans wanted a murder charge. According to German law, murder is considered the act of taking someone's life to cover up another crime, greed, or for sexual satisfaction. In their eyes, Armin killed Bernd to satisfy his own sexual urges and therefore they were sure they could get a murder conviction.

On January 12, 2006, Armin went on trial once again in Frankfurt. Armin told the jury that he had fantasized his entire life about butchering another person for sexual satisfaction and often went back and rewatched the videotape while he masturbated. This time the prosecution stated that it was obvious Bernd was breathing when the knife plunged into his neck. They said that there was intent to kill Bernd for Armin to continue his sexual fantasy. In May 2006, Armin Meiwes was convicted of murdering Bernd Brandes, and he was sentenced to life in prison with the possibility of parole after serving fifteen years.

Today, Armin Meiwes is still in prison, and it is rumored that he works in the laundry and participates in the church choir. Due to morbid fascination, Armin's story has gained worldwide attention with many songs, movies, and books created to share the story. As for the actual videotape of Armin butchering Bernd, it has never been released to the public.

Part Five : Zackery Bowen – California, New Orleans, and The United States Army

"This is not accidental. I had to take my own life to pay for the one I took."

– Zackery Bowen

Zackery "Zack" Bowen was born in Bakersfield, California on May 15, 1978. He lived a normal, happy childhood with his family. He was shy but funny and he enjoyed joking around with his friends and listening to a variety of different music, although his favorite was heavy metal. While he was still a teenager, his parents divorced and his father moved to New Orleans, Louisiana.

It was reported that the divorce weighed heavily on Zack, and he fell into a deep depression. He also suffered from anxiety and worried constantly how others perceived his failures, especially after he lost out on becoming Homecoming King of Santa Maria High School in 1995. However, shortly before his eighteenth birthday, he decided he wanted a fresh start and left his mother's house in Sacramento and drove to New Orleans, making sure to visit as many "party places" as he could.

When he arrived in New Orleans he immediately fell in love with the people, food, and culture and knew that he wanted to live there permanently with his father. Zack eventually got his GED in New Orleans and after his eighteenth birthday he got a job as a bartender in the French Quarter on the popular stretch known as Bourbon Street. Things were going well for him, especially after he met a twenty-eight-year-old woman named Lana Shupack. Lana, originally from Florida, had been living in Dallas, Texas and working as an exotic dancer. She had decided to take a trip with her friends to New Orleans and on the first night out she met Zack at the bar.

Lana figured it would be a one-nightstand, but when she returned to Dallas, she was shocked when Zack insisted the two pursue a real relationship. It was a whirlwind romance and Lana relocated to New Orleans to be with Zack. Shortly after arriving in the party city, Lana found out that she was pregnant with Zack's baby. She also found out that her new boyfriend was only eighteen years old, something that upset her as he had lied about his age. Unfortunately, it was too late to turn back as the two were going to be parents.

Unfortunately, Zack wasn't ready to become a father and Lana often found herself frustrated with his immaturity. Their relationship suffered and when she gave birth to their son, Jaxon, she didn't tell Zack until a few weeks after. However, once Zack held his son for the first time he immediately fell in love and decided he wanted to get his life together to be able to provide for his new family. He took on multiple bartending jobs to support his girlfriend and young son and eventually the two had saved enough money to rent an apartment in Uptown New Orleans. Things were starting to look up for Zack and Lana, and in October 1998, when Jaxon was nearing his first birthday, the couple decided to make their relationship official. The two married in Jackson Square, a historic landmark in the French Quarter.

Shortly before their wedding, Lana found out she was pregnant with their second child – a daughter they named Lily who was born on June 12, 1999. Now with two children to support, Zack decided to follow in the footsteps of his brother and grandfather and enlisted in the United States Army. It was a perfect fit for Zack and his military buddies described him as funny with a big personality. During his time in the army, he was well-respected and enjoyed playing guitar, drums, and making drinks for his fellow military members. Eventually, he was stationed in Germany but returned to New Orleans in the summer of 2001 to recover from a minor surgery on his toe. He enjoyed being at home with his wife and two young children, so he started the paperwork process to move his family to Germany to live with him on the base.

Unfortunately, the move to Germany was hard on Lana who found it hard to connect with other military wives. Zack bragged that his wife was once an exotic dancer and showed pictures of her to his military friends who went back and told their wives. Once the women found out, they weren't friendly to Lana, and she felt ostracized within the small military community. However, their two children settled in nicely and enjoyed going to school there. When Zack wasn't busy with his job, the family often traveled around Europe to see the sights. Even though Lana felt like an outcast, the family was doing well until the 9/11 terrorist attacks.

Zack and Lana both knew that war was inevitable and in mid-January 2003, Zack was sent to Kuwait. He would go on to serve tours in Kosovo and Iraq and his hard work and dedication soon earned him respect from the higher-ups and he was promoted from a specialist to a sergeant in July 2003.

In the book titled, "Shake the Devil Off: A True Story of the Murder that Rocked New Orleans," Zack wrote a letter to his mother about his life in Baghdad saying, "Mom, Hey what up? Not much here. I know, I know. I should have written sooner, but I'm just not good at keeping up with correspondence. So, I'm sorry. Now that that's over, let me tell you how things are here. WE live in Saddam's Vice President's entertainment facility. It's actually very nice. At first, we didn't have anything, but now we've got running water, toilets, showers, hot food for breakfast and dinner, a PX that's open once a week, phones that never work, a movie theater with a big screen and DVD, and all of the other amenities. But still no AC yet. All that's fine and dandy, but I'm never here to enjoy it. I got out every day and drive our LT (lieutenant) out to our platoons and police stations. That takes 12 hours a day. Then, the PLT SGT (platoon sergeant) usually has some other busy work for me. So overall I usually run an 18-hour day. It's very hot here (surprise, it's the fucking desert). Today's high was supposed to be 120 with full BDU's (battle dress uniform), body armor, 30 lbs. of extra ammo, helmet, rifle, pistol and everything else. Well, I've gotta go to sleep so I can get up and do it all again. Love ya, Zack." (Ethan Brown, *Henry Holt and Company*, p. 67).

Things were stressful for Zack and soon after his promotion he received bad news from the base in Germany that Lana was extremely ill. She had been diagnosed with Hepatitis C and the treatment option was interferon therapy which meant she would be injected with the protein to help her body fight off the infection. Unfortunately, the side effects of interferon were brutal – fever, joint pain, low white blood cell count, and hair loss. In addition, the more severe side effects were heart and kidney failure and the possibility of seizures. Lana knew that once she received the treatment it would be almost impossible for her to take care of Jaxon and Lily. Zack was allowed to leave Baghdad to visit Lana but only for a few days. Once he returned, Lana's symptoms worsened but when he asked for another leave to be with her it was not granted. Zack was upset and confided in one of his military buddies that after they denied his request to be with his sick wife he was fed up and done with the military.

While dealing with his wife's illness, Zack was also witnessing the devastation of war. During his tour, he lost multiple friends during shootouts, but the one death that affected him was the murder of a young

Iraqi boy who he had befriended. The boy's family owned a shop in Baghdad, and he would bring Zack ice and cans of coke. To show his appreciation, Zack started teaching him English and the two formed a unique bond.

Unfortunately, in September 2003, insurgents bombed the family shop killing the young boy and the rest of his family. It was speculated that they learned that the boy was speaking with American soldiers and in retaliation they killed the entire family. When Zack learned about the boy's death it was reported that he fell into a deep depression.

In November 2003, Zack returned to his family on the base in Germany, but Lana noticed a change in her husband. He was no longer the happy-go-lucky, funny person she had fallen in love with. He was now distant, quiet, and withdrawn. According to author Ethan Brown, Lana was excited to have her husband back with the family but shocked when she saw the sudden change saying, "There was a disconnect. Part of him wasn't back. There was an emptiness. There were times during close and intimate moments when I felt like I had him back all the way. But those did not last long. It became harder and harder to find the man I had fallen in love with and the man I wanted to spend my life with." (Ethan Brown, *Henry Holt and Company*, p. 87).

It was obvious that the war had changed Zack and he spent most of his free time battling the demons inside his own mind. He complained of headaches and had trouble sleeping but he knew it was only a matter of time before he would be sent back to Iraq. Instead, he started purposely flunking the Army Physical Fitness Tests. Over the course of three months, Zack failed four tests and ignored his superior's advice to improve or be released from the military.

Lana had no idea that Zack was purposely failing the tests, and in November 2004 he was given a general, under honorable conditions, discharge from the military. Unfortunately, this type of discharge causes military members to lose benefits such as education, home loan, life insurance, and even disability. It can further complicate veterans from getting a job as this type of discharge is shown that the member had problems during their time in the military.

Although he was fully aware what the discharge meant, he was not honest with his family members or Lana about how it could potentially affect his future. When he told Lana that he was officially done with the military, the two argued and she filed for separation. She left Germany to go back to New Orleans to secure a job and a place to live so when it was time she would be ready to take the children. Meanwhile, Zack was left in Germany with Jaxon and Lily as he navigated his new existence as a single father and military failure.

In December 2004, Zack finally arrived back in New Orleans and Lana picked him up at the airport. Unfortunately, she delivered bad news as he sat down in the car and told him that she had met another man.

Even though the two weren't divorced, Lana had no desire to reconcile with Zack. However, she allowed Zack to move in with her and the kids while he found a job to support himself. If anything, Lana knew that Zack was a good father, but in silence he was suffering with bouts of depression, anxiety, and the early onset of post-traumatic stress disorder (PTSD). Lana hoped that Zack would be able to get a job that didn't involve bartending, but in early 2005, Zack was right back where he left off having taken a job as a bartender at a place called Hog's Bar in the French Quarter.

Part Six : Zackery Bowen – Romance in the Wake of a Natural Disaster

"If you send a patrol car to 826 N. Rampart, you will find the dismembered corpse of my girlfriend Addie in the oven, on the stove, and in the fridge and a full signed confession from myself."

– Zack Bowen

In the spring of 2005, Zack began working the graveyard shift at Hog's Bar, a small dive bar located on Chartres Street in the French Quarter. The bar was a known hangout for strippers and transsexuals as it was located close to the proximity of the strip clubs where they worked. Zack worked from 2 AM to 10 AM and soon became popular with the women who frequented the bar with his frat-boy style good looks. However, Zack never took an interest in the women until he met Adrianna "Addie" Hall, a free-spirited poet, dancer, and seamstress.

Addie wasn't attracted to Zack when she first met him, but Zack was determined to get to know her. He was immediately drawn to her bohemian lifestyle, something that he had always admired while walking the streets of New Orleans – the poets, musicians, and actors that lived their lives through artistic expression and rejected mainstream societal norms.

Addie Hall was born and raised in Durham, North Carolina by a Vietnam veteran father and a stay-at-home mother. Although she attended high school, she had no desire to finish and preferred to spend her time dancing, sewing, and writing poetry. She believed that schoolwork wasn't important for what she wanted to do with her life. So, she dropped out and cruised around the country, sleeping on friend's couches, and enjoying her freedom on the road. However, when things didn't work out as she had hoped, she found herself back in Durham in the late 1990s and earned a living by working as a salsa and ballroom dance instructor at Nina's School of Dance. However, after a few years, she grew restless and, in 2002, packed her belongings and drove down to New Orleans. For a few months she lived out of her car with a male friend who had accompanied her until she was able to afford her first apartment on St. Peter Street.

The apartment she rented on St. Peter Street was shared by a roommate named Dennis Monn. Dennis, a local playwright in the area, was fascinated by Addie's love of fashion, poetry, art, and of course, her twisted, dark sense of humor. After a few months, Dennis and Addie parted ways and she was able to rent a small apartment on Orleans Street, but the two remained close friends. She worked a number of jobs to make ends meet – waitress, bartender, and maid. She was a hard worker and soon became popular around the streets of New Orleans for her carefree personality and artistic expression.

However, there was also a dark side to Addie Hall and when she drank alcohol, she was known to be abusive and cruel to even her closest friends. Dennis witnessed this one night when he confronted her when she brought two men home one night from the bar.

According to the book titled "Shake the Devil Off: A True Story of the Murder that Rocked New Orleans," Addie was extremely intoxicated and called Dennis a "faggot" multiple times. Dennis would tell author Ethan Brown that after that he steered clear of Addie for three months but later the two reconciled when he realized it only happened after nights of heavy drinking. Eventually Addie moved out of Dennis' apartment and acquired her own at 1012 Governor Nicholls Street.

Due to money being tight, Addie often had to have a roommate to share the bills, but it was reported that she went through numerous roommates during that time. Not everyone could handle her moody side. She eventually took a job as a food delivery driver but when people didn't tip her, she was known to cuss them out and become combative. One of her roommates in 2004 named Rob Van Meter admitted, "When she drank she would get this evil look in her eye and she would just be nasty. She'd say, 'You're a faggot – you like to get fucked in the ass, huh?'" (Ethan Brown, *Henry Holt and Company*, p. 110).

During this time, Addie also dated numerous dangerous men who treated her badly. At one point, Addie caught one of her boyfriend's masturbating to gay pornography and in exchange he beat her so badly she ended up with a broken shoulder. Her friend Dennis said, "Her arm and shoulder were in a full cast. Her face was completely black-and-blue. He beat the fuck out of her." (Ethan Brown, *Henry Holt and Company*, p. 110).

Addie continued to spiral and was known to do cocaine. She would bring drug dealers over to the apartment while Rob slept in the next room and do lines of cocaine in the living room. Eventually Rob couldn't take it anymore and moved out. Due to the utilities being in his name, he had them shut off, which triggered another angry outburst by Addie. When Rob came back to the apartment to collect the rest of his belongings, she refused to let him inside and cussed him out for turning off the utilities. During his fast escape from Addie, Rob had left a pay stub behind, and Addie turned the utilities back on in his name.

One of Addie's closest friends, a woman named Margaret Sanchez, would later say that Addie had been a victim of childhood sexual abuse and because of this she often sought men who didn't treat her right. Interestingly, Margaret Sanchez would go on to murder and dismember an exotic dancer named Jaren Lockhart in June 2012. Nonetheless, Addie Hall's friends all said the same thing about her – she had a "frightening mean streak." Although she craved attention when she went out to the local bars, she also got extremely angry if someone stared too long or tried to touch her. Sometimes it escalated to physical violence. However, in July 2005, Addie finally warmed up to bartender Zack Bowen and the two officially started dating.

Zack was smitten with Addie, and he even told his mother that he had found his soulmate. One month later, in August 2005, Hurricane Katrina was upgraded to a Category Five hurricane and Mayor Nagin issued a mandatory evacuation of New Orleans. However, not all the residents wanted to leave their homes. Zack's ex-wife Lana called him from her West Bank apartment complex and begged him to come stay with her and the kids, but he refused. He told Lana that he was going to ride out the storm with Addie at her apartment in the French Quarter. The two stocked up on essential items including an abundant supply of liquor and beer and waited for Katrina to make landfall.

In the early morning hours of August 29th, Hurricane Katrina hit Buras, Louisiana as a Category Five with 145-mile-per-hour winds. The devastation would be catastrophic as many of the levees failed and flooded New Orleans. Fortunately, the French Quarter was not flooded, and Zack and Addie believed they had survived the worst of the storm.

Although the streets were mostly empty, the two continued to walk around and even gathered storm debris and used it to start fires outside their apartment to cook cans of food since there was no electricity and water. Sometimes, the few people in the area would stop by and enjoy dinner outside in the streets. They were proud of their survivalist mentality and an Associated Press reporter described the people that stayed as "tribes" writing, "French Quarter Holdouts Create Survivor 'Tribes.'" Zack and Addie became the face of the New Orleans "tribes", and they were both featured in a spread written by *The New York Times*.

Hurricane Katrina devastated New Orleans with over eighteen-hundred lives lost. The failure of the levees led to disastrous flooding which left eighty percent of the city underwater with some areas submerged nearly twenty feet. New Orleans was a sort of post-apocalyptic town and there was a surge in violent crime due to people doing anything they could to survive. However, Zack and Addie thrived in their new environment by camping out, rescuing abandoned animals, and serving alcoholic beverages to people in the streets. The media flocked to the couple as one of the faces of "storm holdouts" and their picture was proudly posted in the *New York Times*.

New York Times reporter Alex Berenson wrote, "Some holdouts seem intent on keeping alive the distinct and wild spirit of this city. In the French Quarter, Addie Hall and Zackery Bowen found an unusual way to make sure that police officers regularly patrolled their house. Ms. Hall, 28, a bartender, flashed her breasts at the police vehicles that passed by, ensuring a regular flow of traffic." (Alex Berenson, *New York Times*, September 9, 2005). However, their lives would suddenly shift at the end of October when people started flocking back to the city. Zack and Addie were forced to go back to their mediocre jobs, and they found themselves furious that everyone who had alienated New Orleans during the hurricane was coming back. Zack's ex-wife Lana was also furious that Zack had stopped supporting them and even refused to return her phone calls.

Lana eventually found out where Zack was living and decided to show up at his doorstep to confront him. She was angry that Zack abandoned them as she was forced to evacuate to Texas and take a job at Applebee's to support herself, Jaxon, and Lily. However, when she knocked on the door Zack wasn't home, and Addie refused to open it. Lana and Zack decided to meet in public the next day and she soon found out that Zack harbored a deep resentment towards her. She told him directly that if he was going to see his children that she had to meet their potential stepmother, Addie. At first, Addie was excited to have Zack's children in her life but when it was time to meet Lana, Addie refused. In the book titled, "Shake the Devil Off: A True Story of the Murder that Rocked New Orleans," Lana said, "She stayed in the car the entire time. She didn't want to have anything to do with me." (Ethan Brown, *Henry Holt and Company*, p. 132). Lana insisted that the children should not go to Zack and Addie's apartment and instead he was forced to rent a hotel room on the weekends that he had his children.

Part Seven : Zackery Bowen – Reality Sets In

"Today is Monday 16 October 2 a.m. I killed her at 1 a.m. Thursday
5 October. I very calmly strangled her. It was very quick."

– Zack Bowen

In early 2006, Zack and Addie were back to
living their normal lives. Zack took a job at Matassa's
Market as a grocery delivery driver and Addie became
a bartender at a jazz club named The Spotted Cat. Due
to his notoriety during Hurricane Katrina, and his new
job bicycling around the French Quarter, Zack found
that almost everyone knew who he was. He felt like he
was on top of the world and, as Lana later described,
"The king of Bourbon Street, the king of the French
Quarter." (Ethan Brown, *Henry Holt and Company*, p.
134).

Zack and Addie started going on alcohol and
drug sprees and the two especially loved cocaine.
However, the mix of heavy drinking and cocaine
slowly caused a strain in their relationship and the two
were often fighting.

It was reported that during the hurricane,
Addie stopped taking her bipolar disorder medication
due to shortages in the area during the time and her

lack-of-money. Unfortunately, she never went back on them, and this only intensified her moodiness. By this time, Zack and Addie were constantly breaking up and getting back together. Zack told a friend that when Addie lost control, she often verbally abused him. By August 2006, the fighting only got worse and one night Addie left their apartment with her handgun and got into a fight with a man on French Quarter Street. During the argument, Addie pulled out her gun and pointed it at the man. Although she fled the scene, the police caught up with her at the Governor Nicholls apartment. Inside they found the gun, a bag of marijuana, and a pipe. She was arrested and charged with aggravated assault with a firearm, first offense possession of marijuana, and possession of drug paraphernalia.

A few weeks later, the police were back at the couple's apartment after a neighbor had called about a domestic dispute. The two had gotten into a huge fight with both screaming at each other. When they arrived, they found Zack outside on the stoop and when he went to stand up a bag of marijuana fell out of his pocket. Zack was arrested and booked on the charge of first offense possession of marijuana. Despite the arrests, Zack and Addie continued to use drugs and it was reported that they were going through four-hundred-dollars' worth of cocaine every week. It was also reported that Zack struggled with his abusive relationship with Addie and eventually started going out to bars in search of someone else to fulfill his needs. He eventually met another man at a gay bar called the Phoenix and the two began a casual relationship.

When Addie found out about Zack's infidelity with another man, she berated him and called him a "faggot." She also scolded him in front of his friends and screamed out, "It would be nice to have sex with a straight man one of these days!" (Ethan Brown, *Henry Holt and Company*, p. 147). At one point, she got Zack's cell phone and proceeded to call all the women in the contacts and tell them that he had AIDS. However, despite all the negativity in their relationship, the two stayed together. When they were faced with an eviction from the Governor Nicholls apartment, the two went in search of a new place to live and eventually settled on one located at 826 Rampart Street, right above a Voodoo Temple. The landlord, Leo Watermeier, reported that Zack and Addie appeared happy when they rented the apartment; however, the happiness was short-lived.

On October 4, 2006, Addie arrived back at the apartment by herself and told Leo that she didn't want Zack's name on the lease. She told him that Zack had been cheating on her with another man and she didn't want him living at the apartment with her. Now, in the middle of a lover's dispute, Leo spoke to Zack on the phone. According to Leo's account, Zack said, "Did you just let her sign a lease alone? Because I'm screwed. I'm totally messed up now. She's trying to kick me out of our apartment." (Ethan Brown, *Henry Holt and Company*, p. 147).

Leo never heard from Addie again and believed that the two had worked through their differences. Unfortunately, in the early morning hours of October 5th, Zack and Addie had another blow out argument, only this time Zack decided to end it once and for all.

Around 1 AM, Zack wrapped his hands around Addie's neck and applied pressure, ending her life. In the days following the murder, Addie disappeared from the streets of New Orleans and never showed up again for her job at the Spotted Cat. When mutual friends started asking questions, Zack told them that after their last fight Addie had packed up all her belongings and moved back to North Carolina. Of course, they believed him since he appeared completely heartbroken. One of their friends stated, "This is something that Addie had threatened to do many, many times. She said, 'I'm just gonna get the fuck out of the French Quarter. I'm gonna go to Bali or Morocco and start over.' It wasn't too hard to comprehend that she would do something like that. And she did everything spur-of-the-moment; she was all about doing rash things." (Ethan Brown, *Henry Holt and Company*, p. 151).

Unfortunately, Addie Hall was dead, and Zack was now faced with a harsh reality. After he strangled her to death he continued to struggle with his hatred and lust for her. He would later write, "After sexually defiling the body a few times, I was posed with the question of how to dispose of the corpse." (Ethan Brown, *Henry Holt and Company*, p. 149). Instead of dealing with Addie's body as he had intended to do, he ended up passing out drunk and waking up just in time for his shift at Matassa's. When he returned home later that evening, he dragged Addie's lifeless body into the bathroom and began dismembering her. He wrote, "I came home, moved the body to the tub, got a saw and hacked off her feet, hands, and head. Put her head in the oven (after giving it an awful haircut) put her hands and feet in the water on the range." (Ethan Brown, *Henry Holt and Company*, p. 151).

Zack continued to drink heavily that night and admitted in Addie's journal, "I got drunker and some hours later turned off the stove, filled the tub with water and passed out. I was to be off all weekend, so I had plenty of time to work but due to laziness spent most of that time coked up in various bars with different girls." (Ethan Brown, *Henry Holt and Company*, p. 154). On Sunday, October 8th, Zack worked a shift at Matassa's and went back to the apartment to finish Addie's body. He wrote, "Sunday night, I sawed off the rest of the legs and arms and put them in roasting pans, stuck them in the oven, and passed out. I came to seven hours later with an awful smell emanating from the kitchen. I turned off the oven and went to work Monday. This would be the last day I'd work." (Ethan Brown, *Henry Holt and Company*, p. 154). Of course, the smell of a dead corpse would linger in the vicinity, but no one came in search of the odor.

Zack's last day of work was Monday, October 9th. When he returned to the apartment he was met with Addie's decomposing, dismembered corpse and he decided to use the remainder of his money to have fun and then end his own life. He wrote, "I scared myself not by the action of strangling the women I've loved for one and a half years... but by my entire lack of remorse. So, I decided to quit my job and spend the 1500 in cash I had being happy and kill myself." (Ethan Brown, *Henry Holt and Company*, p. 154). For the next two weeks Zack would drown his sorrows with booze, cocaine, and lap dances at various strip clubs around New Orleans. Zack spent the remainder of his money on "good booze, good drugs, and good strippers" while he planned his exit from the world.

On October 17th, Zack walked to the Omni Hotel located at 621 St. Louis Street and enjoyed a long afternoon of drinks by the rooftop bar. Around 8:30 PM, Zack was seen on the video surveillance camera taking one last sip from his drink before jumping off the roof. Investigators arrived shortly after Zack's suicide and found a suicide note inside his pocket.

The note read, "This is not accidental. I had to take my own life to pay for the one I took. If you send a patrol car to 826 N. Rampart, you will find the dismembered corpse of my girlfriend Addie in the oven, on the stove, and in the fridge and a full signed confession from myself ... Zack Bowen. I scared myself not by the action of calmly strangling the woman I've loved for one and a half years, and then (desecrating) her body but by my entire lack of remorse. I've known for ever how horrible of a person I am — ask anyone — and decided to quit my jobs and spend the 1,500 cash I had being happy until I killed myself. So, that's what I did: good food, good drugs, good strippers, good friends and any loose ends I may have had. I didn't contact any of my family. So that'll explain the shock. And had a fantastic time living out my days … It's just about time now." (*Evidence Locker*, 2019).

Around 10 PM, the New Orleans Police Department arrived at Zack and Addie's apartment acting on the tip received from his note. Detective Tom Morovich stated, "The apartment was a mess. There was moving boxes and junk and crap everywhere; and there were beer cans all over the coffee table to the point where you couldn't see the table. It looked like the people who lived there had just moved in but hadn't unpacked." (Ethan Brown, *Henry Holt and Company*, p. 161). Investigators were shocked that there was no apparent smell of a decomposing body but noted that the air conditioner had been set extremely low which helped hide the smell. When they moved towards the kitchen they found messages spray painted on the walls that read, "Please help me stop the pain," I'm a total failure," "I love her," and "Please call my wife." There was also a black spray-painted arrow pointing to the oven where they discovered the dismembered body of Addie Hall.

Detective Morovich was shocked at the discovery. He stated, "Her head was in the pot and her torso was wrapped up in a garbage bag in the refrigerator. I couldn't conceive of what had happened there. In ten years in law enforcement, I had never seen anything that disturbing." (Ethan Brown, *Henry Holt and Company*, p. 161). Inside the oven were Addie's burned legs that had been crammed into a turkey pan.

Also located on the stove were Addie's feet and hands inside a pot filled with water. Investigators also located detailed notes that Zack had written inside Addie's journal. On the first page he wrote his full name, driver's license number, social security number, and his birthday. He admitted that he killed Addie on October 5th and sexually violated her body multiple times. As for the dismemberment and cooking of her body, he explained that he only did it to "ease the separation" so he could easily dispose of it in different locations.

On page eight of the journal, Zack ended the note by listing his failures in life – "school, jobs, military, marriage, parenthood, morals, love." Before committing suicide, Zack had also used a cigarette to burn himself, thirteen burns on each arm, and two located on his chest. He explained, "Hence the 28 cigarette burns, one for each year of my existence." The tragedy of Zack Bowen and Addie Hall was a tangled web of PTSD, mental illness, and substance abuse, revealing the complexities that individuals can face in an unstable situation. Today, the story continues to shock and fascinate New Orleans and the apartment where Addie's body was found has been turned into a spectacle where you can pay to see where it all went down.

Part Eight : Kevin Ray Underwood – Strange Things are Afoot at the Circle K

"I'm going to burn in hell."

– Kevin Ray Underwood

Kevin Ray Underwood was born on December 19, 1979, and he appeared to be a quiet, yet harmless individual who lived in Purcell, Oklahoma. Growing up, Kevin's mother Connie said that at an early age Kevin started to pull away from his family, especially his father Larry. It was reported that Larry didn't understand why his son wanted to spend the majority of his time inside his bedroom instead of going out and doing other normal things children would do.

Larry told *The Oklahoman* that one incident that stuck out in his mind was when Kevin joined the T-ball team in elementary school and didn't take a particular interest in the sport. Larry said that Kevin "fooled around" in the outfield instead of participating with his team, and when he asked why he had joined the team if he didn't want to play, Kevin responded, "I done it for you, dad." (Johnny Johnson, *The Oklahoman*, March 5, 2008).

Larry hoped that Kevin would eventually grow out of the shy, awkward phase but as the years progressed, Kevin continued to be bullied and humiliated by his peers. On one occasion, Kevin admitted that a group of boys from school held him down and duct-taped his head. It was obvious that Kevin was different and instead of interacting with other people he decided to close himself off from the world. From September 2002 to April 2006, under the username "Subspecies23," Kevin poured his heart into an online blog he titled, "Strange Things are Afoot at the Circle K." His motto read, "Like what you like, enjoy what you enjoy, and don't take crap from anybody," which was proudly displayed at the top of the blog. His first blog entry was dated September 10, 2002, and he wrote,

"Well, it just turned midnight, so it's technically the 11th. But, just this once, I'm not going to get technical, and I'm still going to proceed like it's the 10th. Anyway, let's begin again.

September 10th, 2002. The day before the anniversary of the terrorist attacks on America. And I say...who gives a fuck? I'm sick of hearing about it! I was sick of hearing about it a week after it happened. I liked the coverage of it at first, because it was entertaining. But after a few days of it, it got boring! The same thing happened with the Murrah Building bombing in Oklahoma, from which I live only about 30 or 40 miles away. I didn't care about that, and I don't care about the WTC. No one I know was involved in either of them, no one I know was hurt. And as long as none of my close friends or I are hurt, I don't give a fuck how many people the terrorists kill. I'm not worried about it. I live in the middle of nowhere, there's not much chance they're going to bomb anything here. The only thing I'm worried about is Anthrax, or something else chemical or biological.

They say there's a good chance of another attack of some kind tomorrow, (or today if you want to be really anal about it). Now I'm not hoping they attack, I'm not going that far, but if they do, let's just say I'll be watching the news coverage of it for the entertainment value.

'We'll never forget.' Hell no, we'll never forget, they won't let us! It's been a year people, get over it! People die every day! It's been a year and they're still talking about it! Constantly! It makes me want to kick a hole through the TV every time they say the words "September 11th," "World Trade Center," or "Osama bin Laden." Every time I see a sign, or a poster, or a bumper sticker, or anything else that says, "God Bless America," or "These colors don't run," or anything else like that, I just want to scream, and rip the sign down, or run the car off the road. But I just got a new car, I don't want to ruin it with bloodstains so soon after I got it. It's a very nice car. Yes, I care about my car more than I care about, oh, just about everyone!

In order to protect myself from the assload of September 11th memorial programming they'll be shitting onto us from almost every channel tomorrow, (okay, okay, TODAY!) I'm not turning my TV off of the Cartoon Network (where it nearly always is anyway).

Yeah, yeah. I know my views are extremely unpopular, and I'm going to get tons of hate mail, and possibly be arrested by the government sponsored terrorist group known as the Office of Homeland Defense, or whatever they're called. Because after all, after the September 11th attacks, free speech, and certain other freedoms, had to be taken away from us, "For our own safety," they say. If you can figure that one out, please explain it to me. On second thought, don't. If that makes sense to you, you're obviously the kind of idiot that I don't want to talk to. The kind of idiot that makes me want to ruin my new car.

So, by now you hate me. Good. I hate you too, and I've never even met you.

And tomorrow, when you're watching your little September 11th shows and crying and hating the terrorists like a good little American sheep, remember what Adolf Hitler said: *"The death of one is a tragedy. The death of millions is just a statistic."* For ultimately, this is how the victims of the September 11th attacks will be remembered, as just a statistic. A mere number, on the page of a history book, scribbled on by a bored child. All the loved ones lost in this attack will be reduced to merely this. And I will laugh.

Don't waste your time sending me hate mail. I won't even read it. Just think of me as the 'shock jock' of the Internet." (**http://futureworldruler.blogspot.com/ 2003/01/**).

There were numerous blog entries about his battle with depression, something he admitted he had dealt with his entire life, and a topic he often touched on when he wrote online. He believed that no one understood him as he considered himself socially incompetent, and instead of going out and making friends he would spend hours in front of his computer either playing a computer game called Kingdom of Loathing or blogging. On January 8, 2003, Kevin typed:

"I've really gotta do something. Get some pills or something. I've been so depressed the last couple of months, and it just keeps getting worse every day. And especially every night. I haven't had a decent night's sleep in over a week. I get so depressed at nights I can't even get to sleep anymore. I lie there deeply depressed or crying half the night. I've always been a crier, my whole life. People who know me may be surprised by that, because I usually do not show any emotions, as little as I possibly can. But I cry all the time, not just from being depressed. Sometimes a beautiful piece of music, or a movie can bring a tear to my eye. Christmas specials especially. The Charlie Brown Christmas Special made me cry like a baby a few weeks ago. I don't think anyone noticed, but I was so depressed at the New Years Eve party that most of the time I was sitting over there by myself I was crying. I don't know how people didn't notice, I had tears running down my cheeks at several points. My new coat is tear-stained from it too.

It's the same old crap that's depressing me. I'm very lonely, and no one wants me. I would love some human contact. Even in a non-sexual, just friendly way. I hardly ever touch anyone, and no one touches me." (**http://futureworldruler.blogspot.com/2003/01/**).

In addition to his crippling anxiety and depression, his sexual fetishes also took an extremely dark turn and he started scouring the web for gruesome crime scene photographs and violent pictures and videos of women being tortured. Images found later his computer showed women on spikes being cooked over a fire and graphic autopsy pictures. When asked if these images turned him on, he simply replied, "very much."

It was obvious he was aware of his paraphilia as he turned to his blog on September 29, 2004, and wrote,

"The first blog makes me want to kill people. Speaking of killing people, I went back on my Lexapro today. Not because the doctor told me too or anything, but when he took me off of it, I still had five refills left, so I got one today. I've been off of it since May, and I was doing pretty good, until about the last month or so. I'm still not having much of a social phobia problem, but I'm getting depressed again. Yesterday I was really depressed the entire day. I was so depressed yesterday; it was one of those times where I'm so depressed that my chest hurts. I wonder if that happens to anybody else? When I get really depressed that happens to me. Like usual, the main thing I've been getting depressed about lately is my lack of a sex life.

I mean it, I really need a girlfriend. It's not just depressing anymore, it's actually starting to have a negative effect on my mental state I think. For example, my fantasies are just getting weirder and weirder. Dangerously weird. If people knew the kinds of things I think about anymore, I'd probably be locked away. No probably about it, I know I would be." (**http://futureworldruler.blogspot.com/2003/01/**).

Despite his disturbing sexual fetishes, Kevin maintained a normal outward appearance. After graduating from Purcell High School, he worked at the fast-food chain Carl's Jr. for seven years and his shift leader, Bill Verdan, described him as a timid worker who mostly kept to himself. Bill admitted, "He did a good job." However, he also added that Kevin appeared bored and said, "Just his tone of voice, he just sounded dull. Trying to get a smile out of him took an act of Congress." (*NBC News*, April 16, 2006). Interestingly, Bill, neither his co-workers felt uncomfortable in his presence. After quitting the restaurant, Kevin went to work as a stocker at Griders Discount Foods in Oklahoma City and his odd personality earned him the nickname "Zombie Kevin."

However, once at home, alone in his small apartment at the Purcell Park Apartments, Kevin continued to go deeper into darkness and explored a new paraphilia – cannibalism. In one blog entry he asked the question, "If you were a cannibal, what would you wear to dinner?" He responded to himself and said, "The skin of last night's main course." As the months progressed, Kevin's behavior became increasingly alarming and his hairdresser at Supercuts, Elvira Griffin, reported that on April 7, 2006, Kevin came in for a haircut. However, this time, Kevin asked odd questions about her young son, including a comment about a picture that showed him in a bathing suit. Kevin went on a tirade about men being able to show their nipples while women could not. He also asked if she had any recipes for cooking human organs.

One of his co-workers at Griders Discount Foods, a man named Michael Horner, said that he also had a weird interaction with Kevin. One day, while the two were at work, Kevin approached Michael about a female customer he had seen walking around the store. He turned to Michael and asked, "I wonder what she would taste like?" (State of Oklahoma vs. Kevin Ray Underwood). Throughout his online interaction, Kevin befriended a woman named Melissa Custer in California. On December 19, 2005, a chat log between the two indicated that Kevin had created a shopping list that included "milk, eggs, bread, and human souls." One month later, in January 2006, Kevin spoke to Melissa about his sexual frustration and admitted, "If I don't have sex soon, I will kill someone." (State of Oklahoma vs. Kevin Ray Underwood, 2007).

Of course, Melissa didn't think anything about their conversations and took it as playful, sarcastic banter. Later, on January 26, 2006, Kevin took it one step further and told her that he wanted to write a children's book that focused on anal sex. He said, "Children need more books about ass fucking." He also told her that normal sex didn't appeal to him anymore and he preferred to browse the web for gore and mutilation as it interested him in a sexual way. On February 5, 2006, he admitted he was into "weird and gross porn." (State of Oklahoma vs. Kevin Ray Underwood, 2007).

By April 2006, Kevin's disturbing sexual desires were consuming his life and he decided it was time to take an unwilling victim. For months Kevin had fantasized about what he wanted to do to a child. In a later interview with police, Kevin admitted that he wanted to abduct a child, force them to watch pornography, and then torture them. When asked what kind of torture he imagined he said, "Sticking large objects in their anus and causing them pain that way." He also said that he had purchased long barbeque skewers and planned on poking them through the cheeks of his victim. He also detailed a plan that involved placing the body into the bathtub, cutting the head off to drain the blood, and then placing the head somewhere in his apartment. As for the actual corpse, Kevin wanted to put it in his bed, sleep next to it, and have sexual intercourse. Once he was finished, he wanted to cut up the body and consume it.

Kevin confessed that the sexual urges to torture and murder someone became so overwhelming that he could no longer be satisfied with his fantasies.

Unfortunately, a young ten-year-old girl named Jamie Bolin lived upstairs and across the breezeway with her father at the Purcell Park Apartments, and she and Kevin had become friendly with one another. Jamie liked to come over to Kevin's apartment and play with his pet rat named Freya, and sometimes she would watch cartoons. On April 12, 2006, Kevin decided that Jamie would be an easy target because she was small and trusted him. He took the day off from work and ran some errands in the morning and returned later in the afternoon. He continued to watch out of his living room window for Jamie to return home from school on her bike, and when she arrived, he was ready to make his sinister thoughts a reality.

Part Nine : Kevin Ray Underwood – The Evil Next Door

"She is in there. I hit her and chopped her up."

– Kevin Ray Underwood

Jamie Rose Bolin was born on August 7, 1995, in Edmonton, Oklahoma. Her parents, Curtis and Jenny, separated when Jamie was a young child and she moved with her father to Purcell after he took a job as an auto mechanic. Jenny was a truck driver stationed out of Oklahoma City, and because of her odd schedule, she didn't get to spend as much time with her daughter although the two remained close. When Jamie was ten years old, she and her father moved into the Purcell Park Apartments where Jamie was finishing up her fifth-grade year at Purcell Intermediate.

Jamie was a smart, kind, and adventurous child. She enjoyed four wheeling, singing, dancing, sewing, and watching movies. Her father said that she also enjoyed reading books and she had won numerous reading awards at school.

Jamie also enjoyed riding her bike around the apartment complex. Neighbors would later say that it was common to see the young, freckle-faced, redhead riding around with a big smile on her face. In April 2006, Jamie was especially excited about her upcoming reunion with her mother Jenny. Jenny had been on the road for two months and was coming home to take her daughter Easter egg hunting for the upcoming holiday. On the afternoon of April 12th, just a few days before she was set to see her mother, Jamie and a friend had gone to the local library after school to play computer games. When it was time to head home, Jamie jumped on her bike and pedaled back home to the apartment she shared with her father. Due to her father's work schedule, Jamie often went home to an empty apartment while she waited for him to get off work. Unfortunately, this was the case on Wednesday, April 12th, and it was also the last day anyone would see Jamie Rose Bolin alive.

Kevin looked out of his window when he saw Jamie arrive home on her bike. The two had a friendly relationship and when Kevin walked outside and asked her if she wanted to come in to play with Freya she happily obliged. Jamie trusted Kevin, and interestingly, the previous night, Jamie had ventured downstairs to use a payphone across the street when she spotted Kevin and asked to use his phone instead. He would later admit to detectives that he could have easily taken Jamie at any point, but he had doubts because he believed she was too nice. Now that she was inside his apartment, she got comfortable and sat down on the floor in front of the television and watched SpongeBob Squarepants. Kevin stood behind her and debated what his next move would be. He now had Jamie alone and it was only a matter of time before he acted on his darkest impulses.

Instinctively, Kevin grabbed a heavy wooden cutting board and slammed it on top of the young girl's head. Dazed, but still fully conscious, Jamie screamed, "I'm sorry." According to Kevin's account, Jamie believed she had done something wrong and continued to profusely apologize. Kevin repeatedly hit Jamie over the head numerous times but was unable to knock her unconscious, so he jumped on top of her, wrestled her to the ground, and put his hand over her mouth and nose to restrict her breathing. Kevin would later complain to the police that it was harder to kill Jamie than anticipated and even pulled up his pants during the interrogation to show the carpet burns on his knees. He told the two detectives that while he wrestled Jamie on the floor it was arousing, and he ejaculated on himself. It took around fifteen-to-twenty minutes to suffocate the young girl.

Once Jamie was dead, Kevin wanted to be one-hundred percent certain, so he placed a piece of duct tape over her nose and mouth to make sure she didn't take another breath. He then dragged her body into his bedroom and went back outside to take care of her bike. He wanted to make sure there was no trace of Jamie being at or near the apartments. Once her bike was inside, stashed away in a large, walk-in closet, Kevin went back into the bedroom and stripped the clothing from Jamie's body. He told the detectives, "I took her clothes off, licked her nipples a little, and, you know, kind of smelled her vagina." He then said that he attempted to have sexual intercourse with her corpse but the way she was positioned on the floor made it impossible. He planned on taking her body into the living room and putting her on the couch but realized that she was too heavy to move so he moved on to his original plan of moving her body into the bathtub to be beheaded.

Kevin draped Jamie's body over the bathtub and grabbed an ornate dagger and began sawing at her neck. In his confession, he said that the amount of blood that came out was shocking. He had wanted to catch as much blood as he could inside of a large bowl to taste it; however, by the time he started the decapitation, the blood had started to congeal and spray in different directions. Instead, he turned the water on and made sure the blood went down the drain, although Kevin stated that the clots started to back up the water flow. Not being able to fully decapitate Jamie, Kevin took a break and went back to his computer and chatted with his friend Melissa in California. She would later say that Kevin appeared "unusually happy" and the two talked about squirrels and puppies. Meanwhile, the dead body of ten-year-old Jamie Bolin was propped up against his bathtub, draining the remainder of blood in her body.

With his plan not going as he had anticipated, he decided to stuff Jamie's body into a large, plastic tub with towels to make sure any blood was soaked up. He told the detectives that he had originally wanted to buy a small freezer to make sure the body stayed fresh so he could go back and eat portions; however, the freezer was too expensive, and he settled on a plastic container that he planned to fill with ice. Once she was inside the container, Kevin sealed the top with duct tape and shoved it into his bedroom closet. Meanwhile, while all of this was going on inside his apartment, Jamie's father Curtis arrived home from work to find the apartment empty and Jamie's bike nowhere to be found. He immediately called the local police to issue a missing person's report and phoned his ex-wife Jenny about what was going on.

Jenny was on her way to drop off a shipment in Arizona when she received a phone call from her ex-husband. She was shocked with the news that Jamie was missing and had to pull over on the side of the road. She would later say, "When he told me, it felt like I stepped outside myself," I freaked out, I think." (Chad Previch, *The Oklahoman*, April 8, 2007). Back in Purcell, firefighters, police officers, and a slew of volunteers were searching for the missing ten-year-old. By the next morning, on April 13th, the FBI became involved, and an Amber Alert was issued. Forty-eight-hours into the investigation, a statewide search to find Jamie was underway, and on the afternoon of April 14th, investigators set up a roadblock near the Purcell Park Apartments in hopes that a local resident might be able to provide more information.

Around 3:45 PM, Kevin Underwood and his father, Larry, made their way through one of the roadblocks and spoke to FBI Agent Craig Overby. Larry casually spoke to the detective and even mentioned that Kevin was a neighbor of the Bolin family. Agent Overby noticed Kevin in the front seat, staring ahead and appearing to be nervous. When he learned his name was Kevin Underwood, he quickly acted upon a tip from another neighbor that Kevin might have been one of the last people to see Jamie Bolin. Kevin was asked to step out of the truck and investigators escorted him back to a police cruiser and asked him a few questions. It is uncertain what questions were asked, but it was enough to bring Kevin back down to the police station for further questioning.

Agent Overby and Agent Martin Maag sat down with Kevin and asked him to walk them through his day on April 12th. Shockingly, Kevin admitted that he had seen Jamie on her bike but had no idea what happened after that. When asked if they had permission to search his apartment, he agreed. Kevin accompanied the two FBI Agents back to his apartment and a thorough search was initiated. Agent Overby walked to Kevin's closet and opened the door where he discovered a large plastic tote with duct tape sealing the top. When he asked Kevin what was in the container, Kevin told him that he kept his comic book collection in the tote and sealed it to prevent moisture from getting in. Agent Overby asked if he had permission to look inside and Kevin nodded his head.

Agent Overby slowly peeled away the duct tape as Kevin watched nervously from the other side of the room. As the lid was lifted, Agent Overby immediately saw a girl's T-shirt – the same color described by Jamie's father as what she had been wearing the day she disappeared. The detective looked over at Kevin and mentioned that he didn't see any comic books inside the tote and Kevin immediately shouted, "Go ahead and arrest me." (Underwood v. State 2011). Inside the plastic tub, investigators found the naked, mutilated dead body of Jamie Rose Bolin next to a blood-stained towel that belonged to Kevin. Once the body was discovered, Kevin began to hyperventilate and mentioned, "I'm going to burn in Hell." Kevin was arrested and taken back to the police station for further questioning.

Meanwhile, Jamie Bolin's family was left to deal with the devastating news. Jamie's aunt Linda Chiles would later say, "We were sitting outside his patio door the entire time. I don't know if it's a good thing to know because, honestly, we could have been sitting there at the very moment he killed her and that's an awful thing to think about. That guy took a life that had just begun. Her daddy is not going to walk her down the aisle. She's not going to have babies. She's not going to get married. I mean, it's over for her, and this guy is sitting all cozy in a jail cell eating dinner right now and that's the reality of it." (Ashley Gibson, Daily Journal, April 15, 2006). Jamie's mother Jenny would blame herself and eventually lose her job at the trucking company and relapse on methamphetamine. As for Jamie's father, he packed up his belongings in Purcell and moved to Guthrie where Jamie's body would be buried. Jamie's grandmother Rose said, "There will be too much money left at Christmas and too few presents under the tree. Easter will have one less basket to make; Thanksgiving, too much turkey left over and not eaten; in August, one birthday cake and party will be unneeded." (*Murderpedia*, 2024).

Part Ten : Kevin Ray Underwood – Missing Link Found

"Happy Thanksgiving you Bastards and She-Bastards. I hope you choke on your fucking turkey."

– Kevin Ray Underwood

Jamie Bolin's body was covered in cuts and her neck had deep saw marks that indicated Kevin attempted to decapitate her corpse. During her autopsy it was discovered that the partial dismemberment had cut through her subcutaneous tissue, muscle, jugular veins, carotid arteries, vagus nerves, trachea, thyroid gland, and esophagus. There was no semen found inside her body but there were two vaginal tears that were determined to come from blunt force trauma. Her head was bruised, and her eyes had petechiae – a common injury found in someone who had been strangled. Her death was listed as homicide due to asphyxiation. At the crime scene, investigators confiscated a meat tenderizer, barbeque skewers, a wooden cutting board, a hacksaw, duct tape, a computer, a video about a serial killer, a duffel bag, and a dagger.

Meanwhile, Kevin had been brought down to the police station and gave a detailed confession, which can be found on YouTube, giving investigators an insight into his twisted mind. In graphic detail he described his sick fantasies involving cannibalism, rape, and torture. He spoke about Jamie being an easy target and what he did to her body once he had murdered her. The interrogation ended with Kevin Underwood vomiting. This confession would seal his fate. Meanwhile, Purcell Police Chief David Tomkins issued a statement to the public, "Regarding a potential motive… this appears to have been part of a plan to kidnap a person, rape them, torture them, kill them, cut off their head, drain the body of blood, rape the corpse, eat the corpse then dispose of the organs and bones." (Freya Butterworth, *Medium*, December 4, 2022).

On April 18, 2006, Kevin Underwood was hauled into the McClain County Courthouse with shackles around his ankles and wrists. He was formally charged with first-degree murder. Outside the courtroom, the local community gathered to see the monster in person after the news of Jamie's murder had spread throughout the small town of Purcell. A man named Bruce Shwartz yelled as Kevin was escorted out of the courtroom, "Let's string him up. Let's string him up, baby killer, and hang him." (Mike Baron, *The New York Post*, April 18, 2006). Due to the sheer brutality of the crime, District Attorney Tim Kuykendall was seeking the death penalty if Kevin was found guilty of the murder. Due to intense media coverage of the crime, Kevin's trial was moved from Purcell to Norman, Oklahoma.

During a preliminary hearing, FBI Agent Overby was the only person to testify, and he described what happened on April 14, 2006. He stated that Kevin appeared nervous inside his father's truck at the roadblock and when they searched his apartment and discovered Jamie's body, Kevin was almost inconsolable. Agent Overby described how he had to calm Kevin down before leading him outside to the police car. He admitted that he purposefully left the handcuffs off him because during the time Jamie's family was outside holding a vigil for her and he didn't want the family members to take matters into their own hands. Jamie's aunt, Linda Chiles, would later tell the media, "That was the safest thing they could have done. We would have kicked his butt if we had known at the time that he had confessed." (*Murderpedia*, 2024).

After Kevin was arrested and charged for the murder, investigators would uncover disturbing details not only about his life but what transpired after Jamie's murder. According to reports, Kevin got online the day after murdering Jamie and spoke to his friend Melissa Custer. During the conversation, Kevin didn't seem to be worried about Jamie, only the fact that he may potentially be named a suspect due to his past interaction with the young girl. He told Melissa that Jamie had been over to his apartment a few times and Melissa responded, "Tell her parents this!" However, Kevin responded, "I'm afraid the cops would come into my apartment and see all my knives and swords and the horror movies and documentaries about serial killers on my DVD rack and suspect me." (Johnny Johnson, *The Oklahoman*, February 28, 2008).

In February 2008, Kevin went on trial for the murder of ten-year-old Jamie Rose Bolin. The defense would produce no evidence or witnesses. Defense attorney Matthew Haire told the jurors that he did not dispute that Kevin murdered Jamie; however, he begged them to have mercy on his client saying he was "lonely, very troubled, and reclusive." The prosecution played the interrogation video to the jury in its entirety. When it was over, the prosecutor stated, "And as horrible as it is, that's what you have to think about when you decide if Jamie Bolin, ten-year-old Jamie Bolin, suffered. There is no doubt, ladies and gentleman, that she suffered great physical anguish and extreme mental cruelty." (Underwood v. State, 2008). There was an ongoing joke that it would take the court longer to find a jury foreman than it would be to determine that Kevin was guilty.

Shockingly, after only twenty-three minutes of deliberation, the jury had reached their verdict. Kevin Ray Underwood was found guilty of murdering Jamie Bolin. Jamie's family sat in the courtroom and hugged when they heard the verdict. Jamie's grandmother Rose would later say, "He made his choice. He's a monster in human form." (*Murderpedia*, 2024). The penalty phase of the trial began only a few days later on March 5, 2008. The state produced six witnesses, including Jamie's parents, who spoke to the jury about how hard it was to navigate life after their daughter's murder. Curtis Bolin admitted that after he heard what had happened to his daughter he had to be sedated.

To save their client's life, the defense brought Harvard Medical School psychiatrist Dr. Martin Kafka as their star witness. Dr. Kafka told the jury that the most telling glimpses into Kevin's mind could be found in the margins of his college notebooks. He read aloud, "I can't keep my mind on class. Concentrate damn you ... The computer is taking over my mind ... forcing me to change ... I don't want to ... the computer won't let me be normal ... I'm going completely insane ... I hate this. I'm in hell. I'm in hell. Shut up!" (Johnny Johnson, *The Oklahoman*, March 6, 2008). Another entry described how he believed women and mothers felt about him, "My God ... I'm glad my son does not look like him ... freak ... druggie ... loser." (Johnny Johnson, *The Oklahoman*, March 6, 2008). However, Dr. Kafka said that the saddest blog entry found on Kevin's computer, typed one day after Jamie's murder, was a link to a news article that said, "Missing Link Found." Dr. Kafka admitted, "That was a very powerful statement." (Johnny Johnson, *The Oklahoman*, March 6, 2008).

Dr. Kafka said that Kevin suffered from numerous mental illnesses including bipolar disorder, socially isolating personality disorder, and many severe sexual paraphilias including pedophilia. He told the jury that although Kevin was unwell now with the help of medication, he might be able to once again function in society. Another witness for the defense was Kevin's best friend Christopher Lansdale who described Kevin's time in school and the bullying he faced. He described how Kevin would take the abuse and never fight back, comparing him to a sponge and just absorbing the cruel torment. It was stated that after Kevin was arrested, he was given multiple tests that revealed his dark, sexual fetishes. It was discovered that Kevin had a sexual attraction to children and was fascinated with sexual acts involving urine, vomit, and feces. However, it was determined that Kevin was not insane and showed no signs of psychosis.

After only eight hours of deliberation, the jury returned with their verdict – Kevin Ray Underwood should be sentenced to death for the murder of Jamie Rose Bolin. It was reported that Kevin showed no emotion after the verdict was read. Jamie's uncle Mark Chiles would tell reporters regarding Kevin's statement about how he was going to burn in hell, "I've always said it's where he should go. There's evil in this world. He's a demon and needs to go right back to where he belongs." (*Murderpedia*, 2024).

In 2016, Kevin appealed his death sentence after it was revealed that he had been officially diagnosed with schizotypal personality disorder and Asperger's Syndrome. His attorneys believed that a death sentence would be a cruel and unusual punishment. They also argued that Kevin did not receive a fair trial due to a biased juror and irrelevant testimony. However, the appeal was rejected by an Oklahoma City federal judge. Today, Kevin Ray Underwood currently sits on death row at the Oklahoma State Penitentiary in McAlester, Oklahoma. He was scheduled to be executed on December 7, 2023, but was rescheduled for a later date.

Part Eleven : Donald and Raymond Duvall – Coco and J.R.

"Hell is empty, and all the devils are here."

– William Shakespeare

Donald "Coco" Duvall and Raymond "J.R." Duvall were the oldest of seven brothers growing up in rural Mio, Michigan. Although they were no stranger to local law enforcement, it was reported that police officers rarely messed with the Duvall brothers, and if they did, they made sure to have backup. Most of the residents knew them for their criminal activity – poaching, stealing electricity by wiring into the electrical grid, and fighting. It was reported that if anyone fought one Duvall brother, they would be sure to fight the remaining six later that same night. Tom Henderson, author of the book "Darker than Night" said, "The Duvalls were part of an extended family of felons who were involved in just about any crime you can imagine. No one wanted to make their life harder by squealing on them." (Patrick Durkin, *MeatEater*, December 1, 2023).

Coco, J.R., and the rest of the Duvall brothers were criminal masterminds and everyone in town knew how to keep their distance. Tom Henderson said, "They were as comfortable stealing cars at night, cutting them up for parts, and selling the parts as they were poaching salmon, poaching deer, or tying into electrical lines to steal electricity for their houses. They were nasty criminals without a conscience. They were killers." (Patrick Durkin, *MeatEater*, December 1, 2023). To better understand exactly how the brothers acted, Tom discussed an event that outlined their disturbing and dark behavior. He said one night the brothers held a barbeque with a group of family and friends in their backyard. However, when they were close to running out of meat, the brothers decided to take matters into their own hands. "They got their chainsaw, drove to a nearby field, shot a neighbor's cow, and cut it up right there with their chainsaw. I can't imagine what it's like to butcher a cow with a chainsaw; all the blood, guts, tendons and viscera; right there on your neighbor's property. And then to haul it home, drag the body parts into your house, and eat it? It's so emotionless. It was their neighbor's cow, but they felt entitled to it. Why go to a store when you can take it from your neighbor?" (Patrick Durkin, *MeatEater*, December 1, 2023).

Most of the locals knew how to stay cautious around the brothers because no one wanted trouble. Unfortunately, two men from out-of-town would have to learn the hard way. On November 22, 1985, David Tyll and Brian Ognjan, arrived in Mio to visit one of their friends, Dennis Gallop, before heading up to White Cloud to David's family cabin where they planned to hunt deer. The deer hunting season is popular in Northern Michigan, and every year, hundreds of hunters head to the Michigan woods in hopes of shooting one. Family members would later say that David and Brian left that Friday afternoon in David's 1981 black Ford Bronco and planned to stay the entire weekend on their deer hunting getaway. Despite not being avid hunters, both David and Brian were excited about the trip.

It was reported that when they arrived in Mio both men stuck out, David was well over six-feet-tall, and he towered over his shorter friend. It was also obvious that both men enjoyed drinking alcohol, being loud, and drawing unwanted attention to themselves. Both men were twenty-seven-years-old and had known each other since they were children in the Boy Scouts. They had grown up in Detroit and enjoyed being outdoors, playing cards, and overall having a good time. It was reported that David and Brian arrived in Mio on Friday, November 22nd, and ended up in the driveway of a man named Larry Barker. Larry would later say that it was around 7 PM when they pulled into his driveway and asked for directions to M-55. Larry said that the two men had been drinking and they mentioned they were going hunting.

Mio residents would also say that the two men went bar hopping on Friday and Saturday night. Beverly Pasternak, owner of Walker's Bar, saw the two men on Saturday night. She remembered them because she had told one of her employees to stop serving them alcohol. Another local named David Welch would say that he spoke to David and Brian, and they told him they were staying in Luzerne at Ma Deeters and were looking for women. David suggested locations where they could find women including a bar called Linker's. Once they were cut off, the two men left.

It was reported that they left the bar around 10 PM. However, David and Brian weren't finished and decided to go to Linker's Bar, the same bar that had been suggested by David Welch. Barbara Boudro had ended up going out to the bar that night with her friend Ronald Emery to celebrate his first buck of the season. While she and Ronald played pool she looked up and saw both men enter the bar. She would later say that one of the men rubbed up against her and she scolded him and told him to keep his hands to himself. Author Tom Henderson would say, "They were loud and obnoxious and getting noticed for all the wrong reasons. There's also the usual animosity that locals have for outsiders. So, it didn't help that they made asses of themselves. Locals who saw them in the bars thought they were bad apples." (Patrick Durkin, *MeatEater*, December 1, 2023).

Both David and Brian continued to drink at Linker's and drew unwanted attention to themselves. One of the employees, Cindy Steinhurst, said that Brian had excused himself to use the restroom and while he was gone David paid for his drinks. When he returned, he got upset because he had wanted to pay for them and then loudly shouted at Cindy that he was going to kick her ass if she let David pay for the drinks. Cindy grew uncomfortable and told the owner, Steve Linker, that she did not want to serve the men. Steve would later tell police that he talked to the two men and didn't notice any further disturbances. At some point during the night, Coco, J.R., and another brother named Rex would enter the bar. According to court documents, David and Brian were "acting nasty and creating a disturbance with other people in the bar." (Duvall v. Bell, January 31, 2012). This caught the attention of the Duvall brothers and they decided to take matters into their own hands.

At one point, the Duvall brothers confronted David and Brian for harassing the barmaid and a fight broke out. Barbara threatened to call the police if it didn't stop, and interestingly, one of the people at the bar did in fact call the police but no one ever showed up. According to residents, law enforcement didn't tend to involve themselves with bar fights because they believed they would work themselves out. After having a few drinks, Barbara and Ronald decided to leave the bar and head back to her house located only one-a-half-miles from the bar. While she was in the kitchen, she heard loud noises coming from a nearby field outside her house. She then heard a man shout, "You are dead, you rotten mother fucker." (Duvall v. Bell, January 31, 2012).

The screaming sounds were mixed with the sound of a metallic ping. She quickly told Ronald and the two snuck outside and crept through the woods to get a better view of what was going on. As they hid behind a bush, Barbara said the field was illuminated with the full moon and headlights from a nearby vehicle. Two men were holding onto Brian while he watched Donald "Coco" Duvall beat his friend David with an aluminum baseball bat. David screamed and pleaded for his life as Coco repeatedly hit him with the bat, kicked, and punched him. Coco raised the bat one last time in the air and brought it down upon David's head with such force that Barbara compared it to an explosion. Once David was dead, the men focused their attention on Brian. They beat him with the bat and laughed when he urinated on himself from fright. After he was dead, the Duvall brothers and two of their friends loaded up the bodies into David's Ford Bronco. At that point Barbara had seen enough and she and Ronald crept back to her house.

A few minutes later there was a knock on her front door. When she answered it, she was shocked to see the Duvall brothers who told her, "You saw nothing, you heard nothing. Pigs have to eat too." (Duvall v. Bell, January 31, 2012). Once they left, Barbara saw the men drive off, and the next morning she went outside to inspect the scene. She would later testify that she found blood on the snow where the beating took place.

Part Twelve : Donald and Raymond Duvall – A Symphony of Silence

"You feel the last bit of breath leaving their body. You're looking into their eyes. A person in that situation is God!"

– Ted Bundy

Brian Ognjan and David Tyll were never seen again. One year later, investigators were still mystified as to what happened to the two young hunters who left for a trip and never returned home. David's mother Catherine would say, "People don't just disappear. Everyone says you have to be realistic, but you don't have to be realistic." (*The Argus Press*, November 3, 1986). Worried family members continued to search and circulated missing person's fliers with their description hoping that someone would have answers. It appeared that they had vanished into thin air along with David's Ford Bronco. No one had heard from them, including their friend in Mio who had come forward to tell police the story of how they had planned to visit him, nor had their bank accounts or credit cards been used since their disappearance.

In 1992, seven years after their disappearance, the families had not received answers. There was absolutely no trace of David or Brian, and although they were presumed dead, Catherine Tyll continued to hold onto the hope that one day the two men would be found. In the years following the brutal murders, the Duvall brothers returned to Barbara's house on numerous occasions to threaten her. At one point they told her she had pretty granddaughters so her best bet was to keep quiet. They also killed two of her dogs – one was shot in the head and another ran over in her own yard. It seemed that every time investigators came snooping around, the Duvall brothers followed close with a renewed threat to maintain her silence.

Coco and J.R. weren't exactly discreet about what they had done to Brian and David in 1985 and it was well known throughout Mio that they often bragged about the murders. Coco's then girlfriend would later come forward and say that he confessed to killing the two men but then beat her and told her if she ever told anyone that he would kill her. Tammy Morris, one of the Duvall brother's cousins, would later recall a conversation at a birthday party where she overheard the men brag about beating two hunters to death and then put their bodies through a wood chipper and fed the chopped up remains to their pigs. There was also the story told by Connie Sundberg, a woman who had lived with J.R. during the time of her murders, and she mentioned that around Thanksgiving 1985 she looked outside and saw Coco driving a shiny black Ford Bronco. According to her account, J.R. rushed outside and screamed, "Get the fucking thing out of here before we all get in trouble." (Duvall v. Bell, January 31, 2012).

Throughout the years, Coco and J.R. would drop hints about what they had done to Brian and David after they were beaten to death. Shockingly, it involved a wood chipper and being fed to pigs. However, Barbara maintained her silence because she was scared, and only spoke about what she saw to the police chief, whom she admitted to having an affair with in the late 1990s. However, she would later say that he shrugged it off and told her she used to be an alcoholic party girl and most likely got her facts mixed up. Barbara continued to live with the fear and guilt surrounding the murders. One night in early 1999, Barbara decided to go out drinking with one of her friends named Ruth Fawcett and share her story. She told Ruth what happened that night in 1985, what she saw, and that she had since been threatened into silence. Although the reward with information regarding the missing hunters was $100,000, Barbara wanted no part in it and believed there was no use for the money if she was dead.

By now the case involving the mysterious disappearance of Brian and David had piqued national interest and was even featured on an episode of "Unsolved Mysteries." In addition, psychics had been hired, ground penetrating radar devices had been used, and scuba divers had all come up empty handed. However, once Ruth heard the story she knew it was best to alert investigators and that is exactly what she did. On March 5, 1999, Detective Robert "Bronco" Lesneski found himself driving down Barbara's driveway armed with information that she had witnessed the gruesome murders of David Tyll and Brian Ognjan. However, when she opened the door she wasn't willing to give him the details, and attempted to slam the door in his face, telling him he was going to get her killed.

Detective Lesneski wasn't going to give up and he told Barbara he would spend the rest of his life trying to uncover the truth if that is what it took. Barbara shook with fear as she re-told the story, but Detective Lesneski knew she was holding back pertinent information. So, in order to gain her trust, he began helping her around the house – chopping firewood, fixing the roof, and even helping her install a fence. By now, Barbara's friend who had also witnessed the murders, Ronald Emery, was dead and had been for a few years. So it was up to Barbara to bring justice to David and Brian.

Detective Lesneski hung around Mio and even visited the Duvall brothers alone. Although he was aware of the rumors regarding their violent nature, Lesneski wasn't afraid of them and when he talked to them he mentioned that he wasn't going anywhere until he uncovered the truth. With the information from Barbara, the Michigan State Police and the Attorney General believed that it was enough information to get a conviction even if the bodies of David and Brian, and their ford Bronco, had never been found. They eventually brought Barbara down to the station for a formal taped interview. It was reported that when she was in the room she turned off the tape recorder and looked at Detective Lesneski and said, "You knew I was there, don't you? You know I saw everything." (Patrick Durkin, *MeatEater*, December 1, 2023).

Barbara then told investigators the entire story – the brutal beating of both men with an aluminum baseball bat, the threatening words from Coco and J.R., and the rumors of the men being fed through a wood chipper and fed to the pigs. This information was enough to arrest both Coco and J.R. and the two went on trial for the double-homicide in October 2003. Barbara's testimony, along with the testimony of six others, including J.R.'s son's girlfriend who admitted that J.R. told her about the murders and what he had done to the bodies. In front of the courtroom, she spoke about what he told her and that he threatened to do the same thing to her if she ever told anybody. The Duvall brothers took the stand in their own defense and denied ever meeting David and Brian.

On October 29, 2003, the jury consisting of six men and six women deliberated for two hours before they reached their verdict. Both men were found guilty of first degree murder and later sentenced to life-in-prison without the possibility of parole. Brian Ognjan's mother Helen would tell reporters, "God answered my prayers." (*The Michigan Daily*, October 30, 2003). Today, Donald "Coco" Duvall is housed at the Earnest Brooks Correctional Facility and Raymond "J.R." Duvall is at the Thumb Correctional Facility. Unfortunately, the prosecution's star witness, Barbara Boudro, would pass away at the age of sixty-one in 2007.

In the years following the trial, the Michigan State Police would follow up on numerous tips about the location of David and Brian's bodies; however, they would not be successful. It remains unknown exactly what happened to David Tyll and Brian Ognjan's bodies once they were brutally murdered, but it can be assumed that they were shredded and fed to pigs because, as the Duvall brothers said, they have to eat too.

Epilogue

It is said that the curiosity behind true crime is often derived from the motive of the murder. If we know what motivated a person to murder someone, we can get a better understanding of human psychology and gain a sense of closure when we know the "why" of the events that transpired. However, not all crimes have a clear, defined motive, and we are often left with an extra layer of intrigue and curiosity. It comes down to the age-old question of nature versus nurture. Are people born inherently good or are people born with the potential for both good and evil tendencies?

Note from Caroline

Thank you so much for your purchase. This is the fourth book in a series of volumes where I explore the darkest, most deranged minds in true crime. If you wish to correspond with me, or have any suggestions for future cases, please visit my website: carolinebardot.com, follow me on Instagram @bardotmedia, or email me at **info@carolinebardot.com**.

Resources

Resources – Introduction

Morrall, Peter. "Murder and society: why commit murder?" *Crime And Justice*, 2023. **https://www.crimeandjustice.org.uk/sites/crimeandjustice.org.uk/files/09627250608553401.pdf**

University of Michigan. "Natural born killers: Chimpanzee violence is an evolutionary strategy." *PHYS ORG*, September 17, 2014. **https://phys.org/news/2014-09-natural-born-killers-chimpanzee-violence.html**

Resources – Armin Meiwes

Dovkants, Keith. "The boy who became a cannibal." *The Standard*, April 12, 2012. **https://www.standard.co.uk/hp/front/the-boy-who-became-a-cannibal-6976790.html**

"German court sees cannibal videotape." *UPI*, December 9, 2003. **https://www.upi.com/Top_News/2003/12/09/German-court-sees-cannibal-videotape/27871070981925/**

Jones, Lois. "Cannibal: The True Story of the Maneater of Rotenburg." *Berkeley Pub Group*, January 4, 2005.

"My Dinner with Antrophagus." *Harper's Magazine*, January 2008. **https://harpers.org/archive/2008/01/my-dinner-with-antrophagus/**

"Transcript: 25. The Cannibal of Rotenburg (Armin Meiwes) | Germany." *Evidence Locker*, 2023. **https://www.evidencelockerpodcast.com/transcripts/transcript-25-the-cannibal-of-rotenburg-armin-meiwes-germany**

Turner, Joe. "The Rotenburg Cannibal." *Murder Minute*, 2023. **https://www.murderminute.com/story/the-rotenburg-cannibal**

Resources – Zackery Bowen

Berenson, Alex. "Holdouts on Dry Ground Say, 'Why Leave Now?'" *The New York Times*, September 9, 2005. **https://www.nytimes.com/2005/09/09/us/nationalspecial/holdouts-on-dry-ground-say-why-leave-now.html?login=email&auth=login-email**

Brown, Ethan. "Shake the Devil Off: A True Story of the Murder that Rocked New Orleans." *Henry Holt and Company, LLC*, 2009.

Killer Queens. "Zack Bowen and Addie Hall – Part 1." *Killer Queens Podcast*, March 7, 2020.

Killer Queens. "Zack Bowen and Addie Hall – Part 2." *Killer Queens Podcast*, March 14, 2020.

"Transcript: 36. Bourbon, Blues and Blood | USA." *Evidence Locker*, 2019. **https://www.evidencelockerpodcast.com/transcripts/transcript-36-bourbon-blues-and-blood-usa**

Resources – Kevin Ray Underwood

"'Bored, lonely' man charged in horrific crime." *NBC News*, April 16, 2006. https://www.nbcnews.com/id/wbna12344689

Butterworth, Freya. "The Abduction and Murder of Little Jamie Rose Bolin." *Medium*, December 4, 2022. https://crimesandcuriosities.medium.com/the-abduction-and-murder-of-little-jamie-rose-bolin-725d4fa420a0

Johnson, Johnny. "'I didn't tell him enough,' dad says of love for son." *The Oklahoman*, March 5, 2008. https://www.oklahoman.com/story/news/2008/03/05/i-didnt-tell-him-enough-dad-says-of-love-for-son/61625319007/

Johnson, Johnny. "Witness tells of killer's troubled thoughts, words." *The Oklahoman*, March 6, 2008. https://www.oklahoman.com/story/news/2008/03/06/witness-tells-of-killers-troubled-thoughts-words/61624909007/

Johnson, Johnny. "Woman describes online chat with Underwood." *The Oklahoman*, February 28, 2008. https://www.oklahoman.com/story/news/2008/02/28/woman-describes-online-chat-with-underwood/61627943007/

"Kevin Underwood." *Murderpedia*, 2024. https://murderpedia.org/male.U/u/underwood-kevin.htm

Kevin Ray Underwood Interrogation Parts 1, 2, and 3

https://www.youtube.com/watch?v=uIGPR5cqstM

https://www.youtube.com/watch?v=7-QrxEP2KKc

https://www.youtube.com/watch?v=AtdCzkIjCEI

Previch, Chad. "Trying to live life after Jamie Slain 10-year-old's family struggles to go on a year after her death." *The Oklahoman*, April 8, 2007.

https://www.oklahoman.com/story/news/2007/04/08/trying-live-life-after-jamiebrspan-classhl2slain-year-olds-family-struggles-year-after-her-deathspan/61794116007/

"The Killing of Jamie Rose." *The Purcell Register*, April 8, 2021. http://www.purcellregister.com/stories/the-killing-of-jamie-rose,29903

"Underwood vs. State." 2023. https://law.justia.com/cases/oklahoma/court-of-appeals-criminal/2011/461869.html

Resources – Donald and Raymond Duvall

"Case of Two Missing Hunters Mystifies Relatives, Authorities." *The Argus Press*, November 3, 1986. **https://news.google.com/newspapers?id=nloiAAAAIBAJ&sjid=dasFAAAAIBAJ&dq=david%20tyll&pg=1201%2C118080**

"David Tyll and Brian Ognjan." *Unsolved Mysteries Wiki*, 2024. **https://unsolvedmysteries.fandom.com/wiki/David_Tyll_and_Brian_Ognjan**

Durkin, Patrick. "DEER SEASON DOUBLE HOMICIDE: HOW MICHIGAN KILLERS ESCAPED JUSTICE FOR 18 YEARS." *Meat Eater*, December 1, 2023. **https://www.themeateater.com/conservation/anthropology/deer-season-double-homicide-how-michigan-killers-escaped-justice-for-18**

Duvall v. Bell, 2012. **https://casetext.com/case/duvall-v-bell**

"Two sentenced for murder of Detroit hunters." *The Michigan Daily*, October 30, 2003. **https://www.michigandaily.com/uncategorized/two-sentenced-murder-detroit-hunters/**

Made in the USA
Columbia, SC
24 July 2024